C000161635

C A P S T O N E

Stay Smart!

Smart things to know about... is a complete library of the world's smartest business ideas. **Smart** books put you on the inside track to the knowledge and skills that make the most successful people tick.

Each book brings you right up to speed on a crucial business issue. The subjects that business people tell us they most want to master are:

Smart Things to Know about **Brands & Branding,** JOHN MARIOTTI

Smart Things to Know about **Business Finance,** KEN LANGDON

Smart Things to Know about **Change,** DAVID FIRTH

Smart Things to Know about **Customers,** ROS JAY

Smart Things to Know about **E-Commerce,** MIKE CUNNINGHAM

Smart Things to Know about **Influencing Skills,** NICOLA PHILLIPS

Smart Things to Know about **Knowledge Management,** TOM M. KOULOPOULOS

Smart Things to Know about **Strategy,** RICHARD KOCH

Smart Things to Know about **Teams,** ANNEMARIE CARACCIOLO

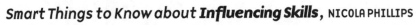

You can stay **Smart** by e-mailing us at **capstone_publishing@msn.com**. Let us keep you up to date with new Smart books, Smart updates, a Smart newsletter and Smart seminars and conferences. Get in touch to discuss your needs.

Smart Things to Know about Customers

CAPSTONE

Smart

THINGS TO KNOW ABOUT

Customers

ROS JAY

First published 1999 by
Capstone US
Business Books Network
163 Central Avenue
Suite 2
Hopkins Professional Building
Dover
NH 03820
USA

Capstone Publishing Limited
Oxford Centre for Innovation
Mill Street
Oxford OX2 0JX
United Kingdom
http://www.capstone.co.uk

British Library Cataloguing in Publication Data
A CIP catalogue record for this book is available from the British Library

ISBN 1-84112-037-5

Typeset by
Sparks Computer Solutions, Oxford
http://www.sparks.co.uk
Printed and bound by
T.J. International Ltd, Padstow, Cornwall

This book is printed on acid-free paper

Substantial discounts on bulk quantities of Capstone books are available to corporations, professional associations and other organizations. If you are in the USA or Canada, phone the LPC Group for details on (1-800-626-4330) or fax (1-800-243-0138). Everywhere else, phone Capstone Publishing on (+44-1865-798623) or fax (+44-1865-240941).

Contents

What is Smart?

The *Smart* series is a new way of learning. *Smart* books will improve your understanding and performance in some of the critical areas you face today like *customers, strategy, change, e-commerce, brands, influencing skills, knowledge management, finance, teamworking, partnerships.*

Smart books summarize accumulated wisdom as well as providing original cutting-edge ideas and tools that will take you out of theory and into action.

The widely respected business guru Chris Argyris points out that even the most intelligent individuals can become ineffective in organizations. Why? Because we are so busy working that we fail to learn about ourselves. We stop reflecting on the changes around us. We get sucked into the patterns of behavior that have produced success for us in the past, not realizing that it may no longer be appropriate for us in the fast-approaching future.

There are three ways the *Smart* series helps prevent this happening to you:

- by increasing your self-awareness

- by developing your understanding, attitude and behavior

- by giving you the tools to challenge the status quo that exists in your organization.

Smart people need smart organizations. You could spend a third of your career hopping around in search of the Holy Grail, or you could begin to create your own smart organization around you today.

Finally a reminder that books don't change the world, people do. And although the *Smart* series offers you the brightest wisdom from the best practitioners and thinkers, these books throw the responsibility on you to *apply* what you're learning in your work.

Because the truly smart person knows that reading a book is the start of the process and not the end …

As Eric Hoffer says, "In times of change, learners inherit the world, while the learned remain beautifully equipped to deal with a world that no longer exists."

David Firth
Smartmaster

Preface

Every business has customers, and they determine its success or failure. And yet it's surprising how little many managers really know and understand their customers. If any subject is worth being an expert in, this is it, whether you manage a department in regular contact with customers – such as marketing, sales or service – or whether your team members rarely speak to a real customer, as can happen in departments such as production, dispatch and bought ledger accounts. If you're not smart about customers, you can't be smart about your business. And if you're not smart about your business, what qualifies you to be a manager?

It's all very well saying you need to know about customers – and it's true – but that doesn't make it easy. Where do you start? That's what this book is all about. It contains everything you need to understand about customers in order to be a great manager; all you have to do is to apply it to your own particular business.

To begin with, you need to recognize that the customer is the center of all your operations, and then you have to know *how* to put them right at the centre in everything you do. This is what the customer service vision is all about, and it is the basis for being smart about customers. But knowing about customers is not just about theory; it's about action. Once you understand the customer's central role in the organization, you have to understand the customers themselves and know how to manage them. You also need to know why they complain, what to do about it, and how to stop them wanting to complain again.

But even that is not enough on its own, because your relationship with your customers is ongoing. As a manager, you need to know how to drive that relationship forward, and keep making it as good for your customers as it is for you. That's why *Smart Things to Know about Customers* goes on to tell you what you need to know about building on your relationships with your customers, and creating mutually worthwhile relationships with new customers.

Finally, what you need to know about customers isn't static. As times change, so customers change. This book will prepare you for the future by telling you the smart things you are *going* to need to know about customers in the 21st century. Armed with the information, the background, the practical guidelines and the tips you'll find here, you could be the smartest manager in your organization. You won't just know the theory about customers; you'll be able to put that theory into practice with every customer you ever deal with.

Ros Jay
March 1999

1

The Customer Service Vision

OK, so we all know the customer is king, the customer is always right, and all that stuff. What more do you need? Well, look at the facts. If every business truly recognizes that customers are its lifeblood – and they are – surely every business should have a hundred percent deeply satisfied customers?

How many businesses do you know whose customers are all one hundred percent satisfied? What about your own organization? The smart attitude to customers is to recognize that you will never achieve one hundred percent satisfied customers, but you should never stop trying. That's what the customer service vision is all about: a vision of perfect relationships with every one of your customers, which you are always striving for.

But wanting your customers to be happy all the time isn't enough. If it were, pretty well every company would have a hundred percent satisfied

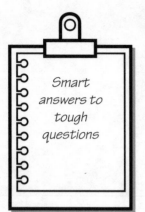

Smart
answers to
tough
questions

Q: What's the point in aiming for a hundred percent when we know we can't achieve it? Why not be more realistic?

A: If you ever reached your target, you'd have no reason to keep striving. You have to aim just out of reach to make sure you improve continuously.

customers. After all, we'd all rather our customers were happy given the choice. Satisfied customers mean:

- happier and more motivated staff, who are being praised and thanked instead of criticized and fumed at

- greater customer retention, which saves the expense of recruiting new customers simply to replace the fallout

- better customer feedback, so it's easier to research the most popular new products and services to develop

- more word-of-mouth recommendations from existing customers; by far the most cost effective way to recruit new customers.

Smart quotes

'A floor-walker, tired of his job, gave it up and joined the police force. Several months later a friend asked him how he liked being a policeman. "Well," he replied, "the pay and the hours are good, but what I like best of all is that the customer is always wrong."'

Sales scrap book

What is service?

The phrase 'customer service' gets bandied about so much these days that we hardly ever bother to wonder what it means. But if we're not clear about precisely what customer service is all about, how on earth can we provide it? It's a useful exercise to run a session with your own team and ask them what they think constitutes excellent customer service. Ask them each to come up with one example of good customer service and one of bad service. Examples are an effective way of being clear that you all mean the same thing, even if you haven't defined it yet.

When it comes to a definition, you will find many of them – and plenty of them are hard to disagree with. But the core of all of them is the same. Excellent customer service is all about giving the customers what they want. Simple, really, isn't it? Well, fairly simple, so long as you remember two things:

- customers don't always know what they want

- all customers aren't the same.

This adds an element of challenge to the whole business of providing customer service, and both these factors lead to the same key rule about customer service: *smart customer service must be flexible*. Anyone who provides a service for customers – directly or behind the scenes – must be prepared to find out what this particular customer wants, and then provide it.

Suppose your team schedules the deliveries to customers. Perhaps you normally deliver to a certain area on a Tuesday, but you have a note to tell you that a particular customer is never in on a Tuesday. If you're following the customer service vision, the smart thing to do is to contact the customer, find out what would suit them, and find a way of doing it. That's flexibility.

KILLER QUESTIONS

How can we provide excellent service to all our customers when they all want something different?

Knowing what your customers want is crucial, and the most effective way is to be able to second guess them – accurately – as much as possible. The better you know your customers the more likely you are to be able to predict what they want; that's the subject of the next Chapter.

Going the extra mile

There's another ingredient that steps up good customer service to really excellent customer service. And that's giving the customer more than they ever expected. Once you are agreed what the customer wants, give it to them... and then give them a little bit more as well. Maybe they asked you to call them back within half an hour; in that case get back to them in ten minutes. Perhaps they want your department to give them a balance on their account with you; so give them a detailed statement. Train your team to look for the extra bit they can tag on before they deliver the service to the customer, and you'll have a motivated team and a happy bunch of customers.

Smart quotes

'If you want good service, serve yourself.'

Spanish proverb

The components of service

So what is 'good service' really about? Although the concept of service may require some thought, the business functions it covers are quite clear. Smart customer service gives equal weight to the business and its systems, and to the people who operate those systems. You need to be smart about both material and personal service.

The business and its systems

Customers expect certain things of you before they even think about how you deliver them. There are clear, concrete, definable standards which you must provide in order to give good service:

- The product or service you sell must do what it claims to do, to the standard it claims to do it.

- The presentation of the company must match its customers' expectations: premises must be smart, brochures and instruction books clear and well put together, delivery vans clean and driven with care.

- The systems for getting the product to the customer – and the customer's money in return – must be effective and helpful to the customer. This means taking accurate orders, scheduling delivery, carrying out the delivery, accounting correctly and so on. From the customer's point of view (being the most important) this means that they should end up with what they ordered, undamaged, at the time they ordered it for, and all their paperwork should be accurate.

Obviously, when you start to implement your customer service vision, you must make sure that all these basic but essential factors are covered by your strategy.

Smart things to say about customers

You can't understand customer service unless you understand what it feels like to be one of your own customers.

Personal service

OK, those were the tangible things. You can measure the accuracy of your order taking or the number of goods which are returned because they are faulty. But what about the less tangible things that go towards good service? The other side of the service coin is all about the personal service customers get from you, your team and the rest of the organization.

Whatever we do for a living, we're all customers too, every day with all sorts of businesses. Always keep in mind how it feels to be a customer when you're on the other end of the deal. One of the things you'll have noticed from your own experience as a customer is that we all tend to

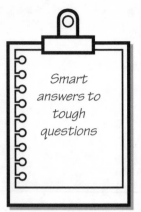

Q: All customers want something different, and some of them are never satisfied. So how can you possibly measure standards which are not only in-
tangible, but aren't even consistent?

A: Some customers are idiosyncratic, but there is always a clear majority
flowing the same way. They know if they are happy, even if they couldn't
tell you why.

judge an organization by whichever individual represents it when we make
contact. So a snotty receptionist makes you feel that the whole organization is snotty. An obstructive and unhelpful delivery driver leaves you with
an image of an obstructive and unhelpful company.

Your customers are no different from any others. Every single contact from
every single customer must be met with a perfect service
response if you want a hundred percent happy customers. Even if a call is wrongly put through to you by mistake, or if the customer's query or request is difficult or
just plain wacky, or the customer is angry about something that really isn't your organization's fault ... you
still have to respond with first-class personal service every time.

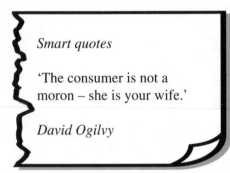

Smart quotes

'The consumer is not a
moron – she is your wife.'

David Ogilvy

- For a start, your staff must be well trained. If you're dealing with a
customer, you must be able to tell them whatever they expect you to
know, and do whatever they expect you to do. It's no good if the sales
assistant can't operate the till, or the sales executive doesn't know if the
price includes VAT or not, or the despatch manager isn't sure when the
delivery is scheduled for. Customers aren't daft; they don't expect the
receptionist to know what new products are in the early stages of research. But they do expect a receptionist to know who does what job,
the names of secretaries and assistants, who is in and who is out, and

what everyone's extension number is. So appropriate knowledge and skills are an essential part of service.

- The attitude customers encounter is equally important. Every customer, at every contact, should be treated in a friendly and helpful way, and as an individual. No one wants to be greeted – on the phone or face to face – as if they are the hundredth person that day to telephone or walk through the door. Everyone in your team and your organization must believe in the customer service vision; only then can they demonstrate honestly their commitment to the customer. This is just as true of people who rarely come into direct contact with the customer. Only if they are genuinely committed will they bother to hurry through an urgent piece of paperwork, or put their full effort into supplying a one-off order.

- Your attitude to your people must revolve around customer focus. From staff selection and training to appraisal and management, everyone must recognize that the customer service vision leads everything. Good customer service must be rewarded above all else, and all training programs should focus on the point of the training from the customers' perspective – how will they benefit from this technical computer training for accounts staff?

'We used to have such problems with dispatch. We'd have customers screaming down the phone at us about a non-delivery, and they just didn't seem to care. Now the customers are put straight through to them. They're better placed to solve the problems, the customers are better tempered and the dispatch people actually seem happier as well as more efficient.'

SMART VOICES

So where do you start?

Sounds great, but how do you get a handle on such a huge shift of attitude? The whole thing about the customer service vision is that it has to run right through the organization. Smart managers adopt the vision in their own departments no matter what the rest of the company is doing, but of course the idea is for the whole organization to think in terms of the customer. Once the customer service vision has become an integral part of your approach, the rest of the organization should be able to see that your attitude is the smart one, and follow suit.

If your team spends most of its time at the customer interface, talking to customers, selling to them, giving after-sales service, it's easier to put them at the forefront of your working systems. If, on the other hand, you hardly exchange two words with a customer each week, it seems a little tougher to know where to start. But the customer service vision is as important in production or accounts as it is in sales and marketing. And this is where so many top managers go wrong. They teach their sales executives to smile and address the customer by name, but they never bother to use the word 'customer' in front of their machinists or their bought-ledger clerks.

There are two key places to start when you decide to smarten up your customer service vision:

1. Analyze your strengths and weaknesses.

Smart answers to tough questions

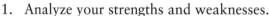

Q: What's the point in trying to follow the 'customer service vision' when the rest of the organization is going a different way?
A: Somebody has to lead the way, and you can't turn your back on the right path just because no one else is going down it. Lead by example, and the others will judge you by the results.

2. Recognize the importance to the customer of every task your team performs.

What are your strengths and weaknesses?

You're going to have to be brutally honest about this, or you will never succeed in developing top-class customer service. At least you don't have to get personal, however. You want to know what, from your customers' point of view (the only one that matters here), are the strengths and weaknesses of your organization and of your own team.

KILLER QUESTIONS

If our backroom staff know nothing about our customers, how can they know if they are giving them good service?

Checkout your strong points

It's easy to forget about analyzing your strengths; after all, you don't want to change them. It's easy – but it's a mistake. You need to go through this process, and you need to go through it with your team, for two key reasons:

- It's very demoralizing to examine your failings in detail if you don't balance the process with a bit of trumpet-blowing. Both you and your

SMART PEOPLE TO HAVE ON YOUR SIDE:

THOMAS WATSON JR

SMART PEOPLE TO HAVE ON YOUR SIDE: THOMAS WATSON JR

- Author of A Business and Its Beliefs.
- Followed his father as chief executive of IBM.
- Promoted adhering to a core philosophy in business, in IBM's case going the extra mile to keep customers happy.

team, and the organization as a whole, need to remember that you have good points as well as bad ones, and that there is plenty to congratulate yourselves on.

- If you aren't deliberately conscious of your strengths, there is a danger that you will forget to maintain them. Just because something is a strength now, it doesn't automatically mean that it will still be a plus point in six months or a year. Only by knowing what your strengths are can you take action to preserve them and build on them.

> **Smart things to say about customers**
>
> The greater the weakness is now, the greater is the opportunity for improvement in the future.

Find the weak spots

Remember, the important thing is the customer. It doesn't matter what your own internal weaknesses or gripes about the system are; focus on the customers. What do they see as weaknesses? *You* might be frustrated that the system requires you to spend eight minutes processing each order when you know it could be done in three, but does it affect the customer? If not, this is not the time to address the problem.

No, the question here is what does the customer care about? By far the simplest way to establish this is to look at what your customers gripe about. They probably don't tell you very often what they think your strong points are, but customers have a way of letting you know what they see as your weaknesses. The smartest way of establishing your weak points is to look at customer complaints. What do your customers tell you they're not happy about? Staff attitudes? Delivery times? Payment systems? Product quality?

You should have a record of customer complaints (and we'll look at this in more detail in Chapter 4). But even if you don't (and you will have before you get to Chapter 5), you are bound to find that you remember regular complaints – your customers don't let you forget them. Brainstorm with your team, and others if possible, and list the areas which you all know need addressing. Although customer complaints are the key source for establishing your weaknesses, don't rely on them exclusively. Sometimes you have weaknesses your customers don't often see. Perhaps you lack a back-up delivery system, for example. As long as everything goes smoothly, your customers will be happy. But *you* know that if ever more than one delivery vehicle is out of action, there'll be chaos.

Once you know what your weaknesses are, in the eyes of the customer, you've still got one more stage to go through. You need to check out the cause of the weakness. Customers always look at everything from their own point of view – they're a selfish breed. And they're allowed to be. If you've overcharged them on the invoice, that's what they'll harp on about, and they'll want it put right. They couldn't give a damn *why* you overcharged them. You, on the other hand, need to know. In the short term, the objective is to sort out the customer's problem. But in the longer term, you need to examine this weakness in the system and find out whether it's down to computer system error or human error, and how it happened.

So if you're going to be customer-focused, you must always look at weaknesses from the customers' perspective. But having identified the weakness, you then need to analyze and treat the cause from your own perspective.

> *Smart quotes*
>
> 'Every human being has a vote every time he makes a purchase. No one is disenfranchised on account of age, sex, race, religion, education, length of residence, or failure to register. Every day is election day … Moreover, minorities count.'
>
> *W.T. Foster and*
> *W. Catchings*

'We knew damn well where our biggest weakness was, even though we'd never had a single complaint … yet. Our computer had never crashed but, if it did, we had no manual backup system at all. There would have been mayhem. We'd just been bloody lucky, that's all.'

SMART VOICES

What's the difference to the customer?

Everything you or any member of your team does must relate in some way to the customer. Without the customer the organization would vanish, and all your jobs rely on your customers, however distant they are. Whether you are answering a phone call or writing an agenda for an inter-departmental meeting, you wouldn't be doing it if there weren't any customers.

The customer service vision means that you have to be able to see the customer's role in everything you do. The customer must take priority every time, regardless of the activity. This isn't possible unless you are clear about the part the customer plays in that activity. Suppose you run the PR department. Every time you circulate a press release internally for information, what does the customer get out of it? When you pay an agency to collect and collate press cuttings for you, how does that benefit the customer?

You've got to be able to come up with answers to these questions – and equivalent questions for every activity in every department – in order to be able to follow through your customer service vision. Suppose someone suggests that it is a waste of money paying a press-cuttings agency to collect all press cuttings, and proposes that you collect cuttings from the national press only. The smart way to assess this proposal is in the light of its impact on the customer ... and you won't know that unless you are clear about the customer's place in the activity in the first place.

You and your team need to work through all the core activities in your department and make sure you know how the customer fits into each one. (There's no need to get carried away – don't analyze the customer's role in turning on the computer terminal each morning; concentrate on the key functions of the computer through the day.) For each activity, you need to ask:

- *How does the customer benefit from this?* In other words, what would be the effect on the customer if you simply stopped doing this altogether?

- *What impact does this have on the customer?* This is a different question, which is designed to determine how – given that you continue with the activity – it affects the customer.

The first question tells you what happens if you abandon the activity altogether; the second tells you what happens if you simply alter or refine it in some way.

Zero tolerance

Why is it that so many managers – often otherwise good managers – behave like ostriches when things go wrong? If something goes wrong, it can only be because there's a flaw in the system. It may not be one that shows up very often, but it is undoubtedly there. And perhaps it's going to show up frequently. Or perhaps it will continue to be rare, but when it does happen it will be catastrophic. And yet countless managers dismiss a one-off mistake and don't pursue it.

This is a daft reaction, even if the mistake is infrequent and not hugely serious. Try saying to the customer: 'Don't worry, you're probably the only person this will happen to all year.' Very comforting. The only sensible response is one of zero tolerance. *Every* mistake, every failure to meet standards – no matter how small – must be investigated.

You don't have to relaunch the Spanish Inquisition and haul up the guilty parties to answer to you. Indeed, more often than not, you'll find that no one needs to be blamed at all. But you do need to make sure that you find out how the mistake happened and, in agreement with the people involved, take action to stop it recurring. Because you can be sure of one thing: if you do nothing, it *will* happen again.

Zero tolerance is the only acceptable approach to achieving your customer service vision. And whether your organization as a whole already shares the vision, or whether for the time being you are implementing it unilaterally, this is an easy attitude to adopt in your own department – and a rewarding one. After all, if you never make any mistake more than once, think how many fewer mistakes there will be overall.

Setting the standard

So we're straight about the starting point for working towards the customer service vision. To recap, you have to:

- identify your strengths and weaknesses

SMART PEOPLE
TO HAVE ON
YOUR SIDE:

TOM PETERS

SMART PEOPLE TO HAVE ON YOUR SIDE: TOM PETERS

- Author of *In Search of Excellence*
- American consultant, speaker and author
- Argues that excellence cannot be achieved without a focus on customer service.

- recognize the importance to the customer of every task your team performs

- adopt an attitude of zero tolerance to any shortfall in standards.

Aha ... standards. That's the next smart thing to consider. After all, there's no point setting off towards your vision until you know where it is – what you're aiming at. You know you want perfect service every time, but achieving it is going to be a bit hit and miss unless you know what constitutes perfect service.

All right, so what *does* constitute perfect service? You and your team need to thrash this out for every main task you perform. You should already have identified the core tasks, and how they affect the customer, so the first step in this process is pretty easy. The next step is to set a standard for each of these tasks. Remember you are setting the standard from the customer's perspective every time. Consider what the customer wants and expects from you.

What sort of standards are you looking for? Well, clearly you need standards you can measure, otherwise you've no way of knowing whether you've achieved them or not. So you want to find standards which are measured in numbers, percentages and so on. Here are a few examples, for a despatch department:

- percentage of deliveries despatched on time per week

- percentage of deliveries which match the paperwork per week

- percentage of queries from other departments resolved within 2 hours

- number of complaints received each week from customers

- number of complaints received each week from other departments

- percentage of deliveries returned damaged per week (you're after a low figure here)

- percentage of deliveries returned as wrongly addressed per week (likewise).

Don't bite off more than you can chew

Now you might think that if you're aiming for a hundred percent satisfied customers all the time, these standards should be easy to set. Surely you just want to aim for a hundred percent rating on each standard, or nought percent for standards such as percentages of returns?

Yes and no. That's the ideal figure – in your dreams. But if you set completely unrealistic and unattainable standards from the start, you will simply demoralize your team. And no one is going to work hard to achieve something they know is impossible before they begin. So the answer is to agree with your team a set of standards which you all reckon is achievable. Once you've come close to achieving each standard on a regular basis, review it with your team and increase the standard. Aim for two percent more deliveries despatched on time each week, or five fewer complaints from customers.

You're working towards a hundred percent all the time. You may never get there, but you are constantly striving. In fact, you will probably find that for some standards you can achieve a hundred percent quite easily, for some you will get there in the end, and others – even if the standard is regularly good enough to set at a hundred percent – will always have weeks when they fall short. For example, it is impossible to guarantee nil complaints from customers. Even in a dream department or company where nothing ever went wrong, you would still get the occasional customer complaining about something even if it turned out not to be your fault at all.

Keep it modest

Have you ever worked in an organization where everyone spent so much time staring at their own navel that nothing ever got done? There are far too many of these companies around. And to be fair, the balance between analyzing your performance and just getting on with the job can be quite difficult to strike. You need to stand back and look objectively at what your doing. There are arguments on both sides.

- *The navel-gazing approach:* If you never measure what you're doing, goes the argument, you'll never know whether you could be doing it better, and how. Only by setting challenging but achievable standards, and then measuring performance to see that you've met them, can you be sure you are giving your customers the best possible service. This necessarily involves a certain amount of paperwork, and time spent looking at figures and thinking about their implications. And it's worth it; it enables the organization to move onwards and upwards, and improve performance.

If a customer appeared in front of you now, demanding to know why you were reading a report rather than processing their order, you should be able to persuade them that it is in *their* interests for you to do the paperwork.

Smart things to say about customers

- *The 'just get on with it' approach:* 'Rubbish', say the pragmatic managers who adopt the opposite view. That attitude leads to an organization of people who never do any real work because they're so bogged down in figures and paperwork. They can't answer the phone to a real customer because they're so preoccupied adding up the figures to see how many customer calls they answered *last* week. Nothing ever progresses or improves because no-one has time to plan ahead; they're too busy looking backwards at what happened last week and last month, and how it compared with the week or month before.

And what about the smart managers? What's their view? Well, the smart manager can see both sides of the argument. Of course you have to set standards and measure performance, identify how you can meet the standards, and then work towards continuously improving them. Otherwise you go nowhere – or your standards shift aimlessly and can go down as easily as up.

On the other hand, the focus must be on the customer. Everyone is there to serve the customer, and that's the first priority. And without time to plan properly, how can you plan improvements that will benefit the customer? It's essential to put the customer first in everything you do.

SMART PEOPLE TO HAVE ON YOUR SIDE:

KONOSUKE MATSUSHITA

SMART PEOPLE TO HAVE ON YOUR SIDE: KONOSUKE MATSUSHITA

- Author of *Not For Bread Alone*
- Founder of Matsushita Electric
- One of the first pioneers of customer service
- Preached that after-sales service is more important than pre-sales service.

So what's the compromise? Paperwork and weekly or monthly figures occupy time which should be given to the customer – but so long as the time is spent for the customer's direct benefit, that's OK. The trick is to balance the time you spend on paperwork related to standards and performance and make sure it doesn't dominate your activities but supports them. And the simplest system for ensuring this is to make sure you don't set and measure too many standards at once:

- You can set up to half a dozen standards for your team's performance which you all agree are the most important ones.

- Once the basic standards are improving nicely and regularly, keep monitoring them but perhaps drop back from weekly to monthly figures just to check standards don't slip.

- Now you have time to feed in one or two more performance standards which you all reckon should be measured.

- Every so often, review how much time you are all spending on recording and monitoring standards, and double-check that it isn't getting out of hand, and that it is all benefiting the customer directly.

Here's a review of the key points to bear in mind when it comes to setting performance standards:

1. Set a measurable standard for each main task.

2. Make them achievable.

3. Raise the standards when it is realistic to do so.

4. Don't set too many standards.

Are you realizing the vision?

Setting standards and measuring performance are vital, but you have to recognize that they are only a means to an end – not an end in themselves.

Who is setting the standards and assessing the performance? You are. And who is the important one round here: you? Nope. The customer is the only judge who matters.

You're going through this process because it's the most effective way of giving the customer what you think they want. (Repeat: what you *think* they want.) But at the back of every smart manager's mind is the niggling worry that they might have got it wrong. This niggling worry will keep you on your toes, sure. But it needs to do more than that. It must niggle you into double-checking – making sure you're right about what the customer wants. The final stage of realizing the customer service vision is measuring your customers' satisfaction. That's the only measure that really, really counts. All the others are simply ways of getting there more easily.

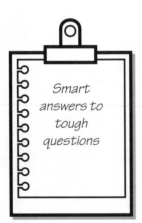

Smart answers to tough questions

There are lots of different ways of measuring customer satisfaction, using questionnaires by phone or post, survey cards to fill in on delivery or after a repair, and so on. You might find that to measure everything you want

> *Q:* If you ask three customers to rate the same performance on a scale of 1 to 10 they'll all give different answers, so what's the point in asking for subjective opinions?
>
> *A:* That's true, but if you ask three hundred customers to rate the same performance, you'll get a clear, valid consensus on the performance.

to, you need to use more than one method. You will find that the shorter the questionnaire, the more customers will respond. On the other hand, the fewer questions you will have time to ask. So aim for a written response which takes three to five minutes, or a phone call which is no more than ten minutes. You may also find that you can conduct annual in-depth interviews with very big customers which last for around an hour.

So what are the smart questions to ask? Well, you need a combination of objective and subjective measurements. The objective ones are questions like 'Did your delivery arrive on time?' The subjective measurements are questions like 'On a scale of one to ten, how would you rate the engineer's manner?'

You need to decide which questions you need answers to; in other words, the ones which matter to the customer. One of the smartest ways of identifying these questions is to survey customers on the phone and ask them what they think you should be asking. You can formalize this further with customer focus groups and similar forums who advise you on what you should be measuring.

Make sure your survey forms are easy to analyze, with yes/no answers, multiple choice, scales of 1–10, and similar answering methods. Produce a regular report on the results of these surveys – at least monthly – so you can keep in touch with your customers' attitudes to your performance. And be on the look out for questions you should be asking and aren't – be prepared to alter and update your surveys and questionnaires. And, of course, as with your performance measurements, the aim is to see a continuous improvement in customer satisfaction levels.

> *KILLER QUESTIONS*
>
> Never mind the questions we're already asking our customers. What questions *aren't* we asking them?

Carry on measuring

Many businesses get this far and then make a big mistake. They take the results of their surveys and then file them, and stop surveying their customers. After all, they've found out how satisfied their customers are now, haven't they, and they know whether their performance standards are giving the customers what they want. Right?

> Smart things
> to say about customers
>
> The function of the market is continuously to raise the consumer's expectations.

Wrong. Customers change. The individual customers change, and the collective behavior of your customers also changes. And you need to keep taking their pulse to know when they begin to change and to respond fast. Suppose you find your customers give you very high satisfaction ratings. Good, you think, we don't need to survey them again for quite a while. Two years later you survey them again and find that, although your own performance standards have been increasing, the customers' satisfaction has dropped by several percentage points. What happened? Things changed, that's what.

All sorts of factors can change but, essentially, if your performance has remained stable or increased, what have changed are your customers' expectations. And you've left it very late to remedy it, if you waited two years to find this out. You've probably already lost customers, and have loosened the bond with many others. And now, you still have to go through the process of finding out where the problem is before you can begin to remedy it.

Why do customers' expectations change? Well, it's usually down to the market in some way – in other words your competitors. And it's one reason why you should monitor them carefully and constantly. If your service remains static while everyone else improves around you, of course your customers will become dissatisfied. They may not have cared that you didn't accept payment by debit card five years ago, but now that everyone else does, they expect you to as well. Maybe your prices used to be the best, but while you've put them up in line with inflation, your competitors held them down. And now your customers don't feel they're getting the same value for money they used to.

Smart things to say about customers

What satisfied someone yesterday, won't necessarily satisfy them tomorrow. The only way to find out what satisfies them today is to ask.

So you must measure customer satisfaction continually. It might suit you to survey customers once a month, or with every order, or on a random mailing basis, or by phone. It doesn't matter which method you are using; just operate a system which ensures that if your customers' satisfaction level alters, you know about it as it's happening, not after the event.

Go back to your standards

It's a complete waste of time measuring anything if you're not going to act on the results. So when customer satisfaction falls below perfect, you'll have to do something about it. And what are you going to do? You're going to go back to your performance standards and see how you can adjust them to fit what your customers are telling you is important.

For example, suppose your standard for deliveries made on time is 95 percent. You might think that's pretty reasonable. But if your customers regularly come back to you complaining about late deliveries, you can only conclude that 95 percent is nowhere near good enough. If this is what

SMART PEOPLE TO HAVE ON YOUR SIDE: ADAM SMITH (1723–1790)

- Author of *The Wealth of Nations*
- Pioneer of free-market thinking
- Champion of market forces in which the customer drives the business.

really matters to the customer, you'll have to put more thought into working out how to improve this performance – perhaps it warrants more staff time or a greater share of the budget; perhaps if you put your heads together you can find a better system which demands few resources. Whatever the solution, the customer should be setting your priorities for you. If your customers tell you that their biggest gripe is late deliveries, you'd better make that your biggest priority.

There's something else that customer satisfaction measures may tell you about your performance standards. You might be measuring the wrong things. Suppose you manage the maintenance department. Customers call you when the product breaks down, and you send someone to fix it. Suppose your performance measurements tell you that 99 percent of repairs are fixed within four hours. This figure has improved over the last year from only 90 percent. But your customer satisfaction measurements haven't improved in line with your performance – they are still poor. To find out what is going on, you have to start from a basic, crucial position. Having accepted the cliché that the customer is always right, it follows that:

- *The measurement which matters is always the customer-satisfaction measurement.*

You must believe this measure, and fit the rest to it. You will generally find that the problem here is that you are measuring the wrong things – or at least not measuring the right things – in your own performance. The im-

SMART VOICES

'I thought we were doing really well. We'd upgraded our new catalogue, and all our products were now illustrated with color photographs. But our customers didn't like it any more than the old catalogue. Turns out they weren't interested in the photos – it was more detailed specifications they wanted.'

plication of the example above is that the customers aren't as bothered as you think about the speed of the repairs. Sure, they'd probably rather have the repair done quicker, given the choice, but maybe it's more important to them that you do it at a convenient time, or that you did it with a better grace, or that you kept them better informed about how it was going. Perhaps these are the things you ought to be measuring.

Measuring the right things

So you're measuring the wrong things. OK, at least you know it. But how on earth are you supposed to know what the right things to measure are? This is where you have to stop looking through the paperwork for a minute. You could brainstorm every possibility, and survey customers with questions on everything under the sun (if any of them could be bothered to fill in a form that lengthy). But hang on a minute – let's be smart here. Let's just sit back and think rationally.

SMART PEOPLE
TO HAVE ON
YOUR SIDE:

PETER
DRUCKER

SMART PEOPLE TO HAVE ON YOUR SIDE: PETER DRUCKER

- Author of *The Practice of Management* and *Management: Tasks, Responsibilities, Practices*
- American consultant and author
- 'There is only one valid definition of business purpose: to create a customer.'

You're a customer every day, in other contexts. If you phoned up to have your washing machine repaired, or a vital piece of machinery, or the phone, or whatever the product in question is ... what would matter to you? Speed of repair would be a factor, certainly. But if you put yourself in the customer's shoes, you can probably think of a lot of other factors which would count for as much, if not more. Don't rely on your own views alone; ask the rest of your team what would matter to them as customers.

You'll need to check your responses with your customers, of course. But, if you listen to your instincts, you'll almost always find your way to the answer far quicker than if you spend days doing detailed research. The next step is to phone up a few customers who have told you they are dissatisfied, and ask them why. This will, almost invariably, back up your instincts. Occasionally it will also bring to light some other factor you hadn't considered.

So now you know what to measure – you know what really matters to the customer. This tells you which standards you *should* be setting for your own performance. And you'll have the confidence of knowing that you're not only measuring performance the right way; you are also measuring the right performance.

So the essential stages in measuring customer satisfaction are:

1. Measure how satisfied your customers are.

2. Carry on measuring.

3. Go back to your standards.

4. Make sure you are measuring the right things.

2

Know Your Customers

The driving force behind the customer service vision is, obviously, the customer. So it's crucial that you know your customers. That doesn't just mean knowing who they are, it means knowing them intimately. You should know better than they do what their buying habits and patterns are, and which products or services they are most likely to be tempted by.

Everyone should be an expert on something, and it's your job to be an expert on your customers. And the better you know them, the better your judgement will be when it comes to developing new ways to improve your service to them. You'll be able to second-guess their needs, whether you're researching new products, finding ways to improve the layout of your invoices, redesigning your packaging or deciding when is the best time to make a sales call to them. It doesn't matter which department

> *Smart quotes*
>
> 'The customer does not know what he will need in one, three, five years from now. If you, as just one of his potential suppliers, wait until then to find out, you will hardly be ready to serve him.'
>
> *W. Edwards Deming*

you manage, an intimate knowledge of your customers will help you to give them a better service.

How can you know all *your customers?*

Some businesses run very profitably with only a few customers, all of them very large. If you build warships or passenger jets you don't need thousands of regular customers. But most of us work in organizations which have more customers than we could ever get to know. And we still have to be experts on them. And there's only one way to hold and access all that knowledge: the database.

The database is the single, most useful weapon you have in the campaign to achieve a hundred percent customer satisfaction. It is the centre of your customer universe. Without an effective customer database, you can't do your job as well as you should – no matter what your job is.

KILLER QUESTIONS

If we don't even know who are customers are, how can we possibly know what they want?

Some organizations have excellent databases, and some have ones which are pretty useless. You may not be in a position to choose your own organization's database, but it's worth knowing what constitutes an effective one. That way, you'll at least know what knowledge you're missing (assuming there are flaws in the system you work with), and you'll be in a position to agitate for improvements. And if an opportunity to upgrade the system comes along, you'll be able to put forward a practical and well argued proposal for the changes you need so that you and your team – and the rest of the organization – can work more effectively towards the customer service vision.

- The first, crucial criterion for an effective database is that it must be fully integrated with all departments. It's no good if the accounts department use their own system which doesn't interrelate with anyone else's, or if sales and despatch are using different databases.

Just imagine phoning a customer to query an unpaid account, only to discover that they are deep in dispute with your sales department over being sent the wrong order in the first place. An integrated database would have alerted you to this before you picked up the phone; with separate records you'll make a fool of yourself and your organization when you get through to the customer.

- You need to be able to access the information on the database easily. And although you may be able to access it through any one of several routes, the primary access should be by customer name. It's the customers who call the shots round here, and they are the ones that count. It's very hard to focus yourself fully on the customer if every time you want to know anything about them you turn to your computer terminal and key in a number or a transaction code.

If your organization is customer-driven, the customer personally must be your main access to your records. It is, of course, a useful option to be able to access information by other criteria – order date, product or whatever – but these are not the search criteria for which the system should be set up.

> *Smart things to say about customers*
>
> We can't give our customers the best service without the information we have stored, but unless we use it wisely the information in itself is worthless.

- OK, so the primary access should be by customer name. But you should be able to access information by any search criteria. You want to be able to find out how your customers behave, and to cross-reference different behaviors. Do the customers who place the most orders with you actually spend above average, or are they placing lots of small orders? If you search your database by number of orders *and* by total annual spend, you can find the answer to this question.

To give you a couple more examples: is there a correlation between late payers and frequent complainers? Are most of the late deliveries in one or two particular geographical regions? This is the kind of information which can help you to solve customers problems or find new and better methods of customer service. But you can only find the answers if you have a database which will allow you to access it by any search criteria.

So those are the three key features of an effective database:

- it should be integrated;

- it should be organized by customer name; and

- you should be able to access it by any criteria.

So *what goes on the database?*

It should be obvious that the more information you put onto your database, the more information you can get off it. So you need to make sure that your database is set up to hold as much useful information as possible. It's pointless just holding a computerised list of customers – you might as well have a manual card index system. You can't give great service on that sort of basis. If you're going to know your customers intimately, you want to hold as much information as possible on them.

If you sell direct to consumers, for example, you'll need to record their ages. Perhaps certain products only really sell to the under 30s. If you don't know this, you'll most probably keep trying to persuade the over 50s to buy them. This not only costs you money; it also costs you a degree of closeness in your relationship with the customer. You must know yourself that when you see an ad or receive a piece of mail offering you something which you'd never want, it makes you feel 'these people don't have a clue about me'. If your customers are going to feel that you really understand them, you need detailed information to be able to demonstrate as much.

OK, so you won't be able to put every last piece of information on your database immediately you enter a new customer; you won't have it all straight away. But you should be able to build it up over time, and we'll take a closer look at that later on. Assuming your database lists prospects as well as customers, you will have fewer details about these than about existing customers. But you should aim to build up information over time.

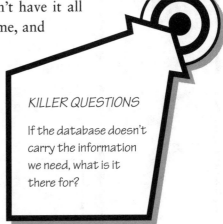

KILLER QUESTIONS

If the database doesn't carry the information we need, what is it there for?

And another thing. It should be possible for you personally to add information which you feel should be included and isn't. Any manager who sees a use for a particular type of information should be able to research the information and then add it to the database.

As you look through the following lists of categories of information which your database could include, you should get a picture of the kind of information your organization should be holding on each of its customers. This is the knowledge that you need as a basis for providing top-class customer service. The smart manager's skill is in understanding how to make the most of this knowledge in furthering the standards of customer service in their department and in the organization as a whole.

There are four basic categories of information to include on any well planned database:

- personal details

- address details

- financial details

- customer (or prospect) history.

Some of these vary depending on whether your customers are businesses or consumers, as you'll see in the lists below. You also need to know, as a manager, about the Data Protection Act. If you store more than a person's name and address on a computer, you must register with the Data Protection Registrar. You are also obliged to disclose to the person what infor-

SMART PEOPLE
TO HAVE ON
YOUR SIDE:

GARY HAMEL

SMART PEOPLE TO HAVE ON YOUR SIDE: GARY HAMEL

- Co-author of *Competing for the Future*
- American academic and strategic consultant
- Believes in a new vision for developing strategy.

mation you hold on them if they ask, and there are restrictions on divulging the information, for example when selling mailing lists.

Personal details

So what is all this personal information you want about your customers? Not every database needs to hold all the details below, but you will probably benefit from having most of them on yours. Your organization may well have the capability to hold all the information but hasn't actually bothered to enter it onto the system; sadly this is often the case. If so, the smart thing to do is to add all the information you could possibly need, and let everyone see how much better the customers are served if you know more about them.

So here's a guide to the kind of personal information you want to have about each of your customers and prospects:

Smart things to say about customers

The more intimately we know our customers, the more precisely we will be able to offer them exactly what they want.

- name

- age

- marital status

- number of children

- employment status (professional, white collar etc.)

- income bracket

- type of job (civil servant, media etc.)

- credit status.

Your database will presumably use codes for some of these categories, such as income bracket, employment status and the like. The kind of personal information you should hold on business customers and prospects will look more like this:

- name

- job description

- department or section

- direct phone number

- direct fax number

- e-mail address

- job code (sales, production etc.)

- authorizer (i.e. ultimate buying decision maker)

- personal address data.

You should be starting to recognize the huge knowledge of your customers which the database can give you; and we've only just started.

Smart
answers to
tough
questions

Q: How can we justify the cost of a system so big it does virtually everything, even when we're not sure exactly what we need it to do?
A: How can we justify any system at all which doesn't give us the flexibility to be able to improve service to our customers, and keep improving it?

Address details

This category of information enables you to make contact with your customers, and to analyze the information in terms of location. We'll start with consumer data:

- full address

- phone number

- fax number

- e-mail address

- type of property (rural or urban, detached, terraced, own, rented, etc.)

- regional code (north west, London area etc.)

- sales area (if you divide locations into your own administrative areas)

- media area code (TV or newspaper advertising regions).

Once again, businesses demand a slightly different set of data:

- full company name

- shortened version of company name

- full address

- switchboard phone number

- main fax number

- e-mail address

- telex number

- company type (parent company, independent, sole trader etc.)

- parent company name, address and main phone number

- regional code

- type of business (industrial, retail etc.)

- principal products or services

- importer and exporter indicators

- number of employees bracket

- turnover bracket.

Financial details

The next category of data tells you all about the way your customers spend money with you. If you don't record this data, you have no way of accessing this vital knowledge:

- type of account

- date of first order

- most recent order date

- average order value

- average payment time.

This kind of knowledge enables you to promote products you know your customers are likely to be prepared to pay for, or make special offers to selected customers as a bonus for prompt payment.

Customer or prospect history

So far you've got loads of information about the customer themselves, but precious little about your relationship with them. But customer service is all about recognizing the relationship and letting the customer know that you are aware of your history together. This last section of data records your interactions with the customer.

Imagine you're on the phone to a customer, and you have their details up on the computer screen in front of you as you speak. You can confirm with them the date of their last order, refer back to purchases they made last year, or check they were happy with the replacement part they were sent last month. These are the kinds of things which make customers feel wanted and understood; the precise factors which make for smart customer service:

> You wouldn't conduct a conversation with a partner or friend as if they were a stranger, without acknowledging the shared relationship you have had in the past; so treat your customers with the same respect.

Smart things to say about customers

- type of contacts from customer or prospect by code (orders, enquiries, responses to surveys, visits to exhibitions etc.)

- date of each contact

- value of contact

- method of contact (phone, fax, post etc.)

- details of any late deliveries, complaints, disputes etc.

- date and type of all contacts initiated by your organization (mailings, phone calls, invitations to events or exhibitions etc.).

This information is also valuable for another reason. When you survey customers and prospects, they may give you all sorts of information about what they might buy, or what sort of service they would expect. But, although they are most probably giving you this information in good faith, what people say they will do, and what they actually do, are not always the same thing. But this part of your database tells you specifically what your customers and prospects have actually demonstrated that they do – how much they spend, how often they order, whether they turn up to exhibitions and so on.

These lists should be fairly exhaustive, but every organization has its own particular requirements which may not be typical. So you might need to add certain other categories to your database.

SMART VOICES	'I was on the phone to this customer, making a routine call to check they were happy with last week's order. It turned out it had never arrived and they were having an ongoing fight with dispatch about it. Nobody had told me! I just wanted to curl up and disappear.'

But it should be clear now what knowing your customers is all about. You should know about them, their circumstances, their finances and their relationship with you. And the point of all this is not to be nosy, but to provide them with better service. If you're smart, you can use this knowledge (as we'll see in the next chapter) to design offers and services which suit your customers perfectly. And the basis of all this knowledge – the only kind of basis that really works – is an effective database.

Smart quotes

'The first step in getting ahead is to listen.'

Liam Strong

And as we'll see in Chapter 6, your database is the foundation for relationship marketing in the digital marketplace of the 21st century. Doing business on the Internet relies on a large and flexible databse.

Building your database

That all sounded pretty straightforward. But it's one thing knowing what you want on your database, and quite another actually getting the information on there. But get it on there you must. Some companies collect masses of data and then never get round to entering it. But if you don't enter the information you collect, you have gained nothing and you have wasted all the money you spent collecting it. If you *do* enter it, you should have gained far more value than the cost of acquiring it. So the smart approach is to make sure that everything gets entered, and that the time and cost of enter-

SMART PEOPLE
TO HAVE ON
YOUR SIDE:

AKIO MORITA

SMART PEOPLE TO HAVE ON YOUR SIDE: AKIO MORITA

- Japanese businessman and co-founder of Sony.
- Co-author of *Made in Japan*.
- Pioneer in creating new markets.

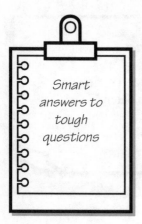

Smart
answers to
tough
questions

Q: Get real! How can you possibly find the staff time to enter every little piece of data you have onto the computer?

A: What is the point of having data at all if you don't exploit all the information you've got? And if data is entered regularly and as a routine it takes up very little time.

ing information is budgeted for as part of the whole project of collecting it. So where are you getting all this data from? There are two obvious sources:

- information which comes to you

- information which you go out and get.

Information about orders, queries and so on tends to arrive with you when the customer makes contact, and often brings incidental information with it. Any other missing data you can aim to go out and collect through surveys, questionnaires or buying in data.

Data which comes to you

Every time a new prospect gets in touch with you, in response to an advertisement or through visiting an exhibition stand, or simply by phoning up on recommendation, you will collect information from them. They may not be over-keen to volunteer their age or income on a first phone call, but you can at least ask for their name, address and phone number.

SMART VOICES

'I used to worry it might sound rude to ask questions on a first contact, but since I started doing it I find that prospects and customers like it – they want you to be interested in them.'

When regular customers make contact, you can ask for all sorts of other information from them. Most of this should be acquired as standard on a first order, but it is a smart policy to ask everyone in your team to fill on the 'blanks' on the database any time they get the chance. If you call a business customer about an order and notice that you don't have their direct phone number, or their e-mail address, simply say 'Do you have a direct line? We don't seem to have any record of the number.'

Ideally, everyone in the organization should adopt this approach. If despatch are calling about a delivery query, or accounts take a call about payment terms, they can still ask for missing information. Obviously the more sensitive data can't be collected in this way, but a great deal of information can and should be.

Customer – or prospect – history should also be entered onto the database. Straight orders, and certain other transactions and contacts, are presumably entered on to the computer automatically. But suppose you send out invitations to a new product launch, or welcome visitors to your exhibition stand. Make sure that the database holds a record of the fact under each customer who was invited, and whether they turned up or not. This should be a standard, budgeted part of the job of inviting customers to events.

KILLER QUESTIONS

Unless everyone in the organization is responsible for building up the data store, how can everyone feel involved in using it and getting the best from it?

There is some survey information which in effect comes to you. If you conduct continuous surveys, such as a card which goes out with every delivery, this data will constantly come back to you. Once again, there's no point in the exercise unless you enter the results so that you can use them. As well as the responses themselves, you'll find it's extremely useful to have a record of who does and doesn't respond to surveys – most people are either generally predisposed to or virtually never do.

So you can assemble a huge amount of data without going anywhere:

- from new prospects

- from contact with existing customers

- by entering all customer and prospect history on to the database

- by processing regular, ongoing surveys.

Data you have to go and get

I'm afraid you can't just sit back and wait for all the data you need: all this will still leave some gaps. Your sections of data on financial details and on customer history should be complete if you and your team, and the rest of the organization, are doing their jobs properly. But the personal and address details may still be incomplete. If you need this data in order to run your department effectively – don't worry. You can still get hold of it.

If you need to find out data about your customers which you don't have internally, the answer is simple: you'll have to go and ask them. If data is

Q: Just because you ask your prospects or customers for personal information, how do you know they'll give it to you?
A: You don't. But if you *don't* ask them, you can be certain they *won't* give it to you.

missing on only a few customers you may be able to conduct this research by phone. Otherwise you'll need to send out a postal questionnaire. If your database can cope with the data but it has never been collected and entered, you are going to have to mail a lot of customers to remedy the situation.

Your best bet is to hire an agency to do this for you. It is almost always the most cost-effective approach, and they have the necessary skills. Bear in mind that not everyone will respond by any means; a good agency will know how to maximize the response rate. Although you should aim, within reason, to complete as many database entries as possible, this is not actually essential. The value of this kind of information tends to be collective rather than individual. So long as you know the ages, for example, of a good percentage of your customers, you can quite easily establish which age brackets tend to behave in certain ways. This information will then apply to all your customers. Of course, if you want to send a special offer to the under 30s, you still need to know who they are. But the information you collect isn't useless if it isn't complete across the database; it simply increases in value as its coverage of the database increases.

One other thing you may be wondering about: what about all those personal questions such as income brackets and so on? Can you seriously just ask them straight out? Well, yes you can, so long as you are diplomatic:

- Ask more personal questions towards the end of the questionnaire (or telephone survey).

- Include a covering letter (or an introduction on the phone) explaining why answering the questionnaire, and telling you more about themselves, will enable you to give the customer a better service in the future.

Getting a result

Certain dumb managers are of the opinion that they can do everything; the smart manager knows that their skill is often in knowing when to bring in the experts. But even if you are smart enough to employ an agency to conduct your research, you should still need to know for yourself some of the tricks of the trade for maximizing the response to a questionnaire. So here are some really smart things to know about customers:

- The more contact you have with customers the more likely they are to respond, so expect the highest response from regular customers and the lowest from prospects.

- Customers are more likely to return your questionnaire if you send them a covering letter explaining how doing so will benefit them.

- Customers are more likely to respond if the covering letter is personalized.

- An incentive for answering will increase the response rate – a discount, a free gift, entry in a prize draw or something of the sort.

- You can up the response rate by sending out a reply-paid envelope.

- Send a reminder letter with another copy of the questionnaire to anyone who hasn't replied after about 10 days to 2 weeks.

- As a general guide, send out questionnaires to business customers on a Monday; they'll get binned if they arrive at the end of the week. Questionnaires to consumers should go out on a Thursday so they can be filled in over the weekend.

Knowledge that doesn't make it to the database

Although, as we have already seen, the database is the central fund of knowledge about your customers, don't make the common mistake of thinking it is the only source. All the information on your database is essentially factual and quantitative. But you also want to know your customers' thoughts, feelings, opinions and predictions for the future. You cannot analyze these in a way which can be entered onto a computer using field codes.

Qualitative research

The smart manager is always up-to-date on the less quantitative aspects of customer knowledge, and has a feel for changes and altered expectations as a result. One of the ways of keeping a finger on the customer's pulse is to conduct qualitative research – either alongside the quantitative research you are running to update your database, or as a completely separate exercise.

Qualitative research is harder to analyze in bulk, but it often doesn't need to be analyzed in detail. And sometimes it's well worth the effort. You might employ an agency to do the research and report on it for you, or you might do it very informally. In the long term – if you're smart – you'll do both at different times.

Formal research

This entails a structured questionnaire, either by phone or post, asking questions which do not demand yes/no answers, but which require thoughts and opinions in response. There is a great skill to designing this kind of questionnaire effectively, and if you have any sense you'll bring in an expert to help.

You must have a report at the end of this research so that you, and your fellow managers, can get the benefit of the findings. However, you will find that it helps enormously to read through some of the response forms individually, even if you only have time to look at a proportion of them. After all, your customers are all individuals, and you get a better feel for this if you look at their responses individually as well as collectively.

Qualitative research is generally valid with a smaller sample than quantitative research. You may well find that a survey group of only about twenty or thirty customers gives you a useful result. You can also choose quite small samples for specific purposes for this kind of research – only your top 50 customers, for example, or only those who have made a complaint within the last two months.

One particularly useful sample group is 'live' customers; in other words those who are currently engaged in a transaction, between ordering and

KILLER QUESTIONS

If we want to know what our customers are thinking, why hold meetings and commission reports? Why not just ask them?

Smart things to say about customers

The more specialized the research, the smaller the sample you can usefully survey. (Even if you survey a higher proportion, the actual numbers go down.) If you want to know how a thousand customers think or behave, you need to ask at least fifty of them. If you want to know how only fifty customers typically think, you only need to ask ten.

delivery. This is a special group, since you can argue that all other customers are past or future customers, but these are the only truly current ones.

Informal research

Informal research is equally valid, and smart managers conduct it themselves as well as delegating it. Every time you chat with a customer over the phone or at your exhibition stand, you have the opportunity to run this kind of research. Rather than holding aimless discussions, or talking about last year's holidays, have a mental list of questions (and make sure your team have them too) to ask these customers or prospects.

This is the kind of thing that puts you several steps ahead of the dumb managers who are still talking about last year's holidays and *think* that means that they know the customer better than you do. They don't know the things which matter about the customer – in other words they aren't learning about their custom – while you are busy finding out how the customer sees the product developing, or what improvements they would like to see in customer service.

You can also conduct informal research over the phone. You might, perhaps, call up two 'live' customers a week with a few questions, for which you would record the responses and produce a regular update report.

Keeping informed

And there's more. Another essential part of getting to know your customers

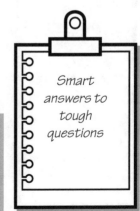

Smart answers to tough questions

> Q: As a manager, how can you afford the time to conduct your own research, however formal? That task can be delegated to your team.
> A: As a manager, who can I better afford the time to talk to than customers? When I talk to a customer, I'm talking to the boss.

is simply being well read on the subject. Smart managers read the trade press, they listen to radio programs, they get hold of industry reports, they watch television programs, they read relevant articles in the national press, they check out their competitors' annual reports and brochures, and there isn't a thing that goes on in the industry which they don't know about.

This kind of background information-gathering may not have the directness of conversing with a customer, but it is essential to give the customer a contact. You can't comment on whether a friend should buy a particular pair of shoes if you haven't seen the outfit they're intended to go with; you wouldn't form an opinion of a car if you'd only seen the engine and chassis with all the bodywork stripped off. And equally, you cannot understand what makes your customers tick if you don't also understand the world they operate in.

If you sell beauty products to young, professional women, read *Cosmopolitan* magazine, at least occasionally. If your organization manufactures commercial kitchen equipment, subscribe to *Caterer and Hotelkeeper*. Learn everything you can about the world your customers move in; the smart thing to know about customers is that you *really* have to know about them.

SMART PEOPLE
TO HAVE ON
YOUR SIDE:

ALAN SUGAR

SMART PEOPLE TO HAVE ON YOUR SIDE: ALAN SUGAR

- Founder of Amstrad.
- Dedicated to the philosophy of creating profits by giving customers whatever they want.

The forgotten customers

Although it might sound strange at first, many organizations have customers who aren't on their database and have never placed an order. All too often they get forgotten by dumb managers. They are your customers' customers. Sometimes, in a complex manufacturing chain, there may be a series of these. If you sell to retailers, the end consumer is as important to you as the retailer. If they stop buying, the retailer stops buying from you. If they want more, the retailer's order with you goes up.

You need to learn who these customers further down the line are and, in a complex chain, you need to know who are the key decision makers and who has the most important influence on buying patterns. Then learn about these customers.

The best source of information is your own immediate customer. It is in their interests for you to be an expert on *their* customers, and they will see it as good service to them that you take the trouble to learn about their world. So regular conversations, and formal and informal research, should be easy to arrange and get a good response from your customers. But don't stop there.

'My organization sells components to washing machine manufacturers. I used to think about the end customers in the chain and, I'm embarrassed to admit, it was a fair while before it clicked that I was trying to imagine myself.'

SMART VOICES

You still need to read the right papers and trade magazines, look at industry reports, listen to and watch relevant broadcasts, and get hold of the end customers' annual reports and brochures. Just because these customers are at one – or more – remove, doesn't make them any less important to you.

The decision makers

And there's another category of forgotten customers: the decision makers. If you have a business customer who needs authorization for large purchases, you probably know about it. But consumers often buy only on the advice of others. Let's get sexist here for a moment: many men will not buy a suit or a tie without the OK from their partner. Many women won't buy a car unless their husband or boyfriend approves it. And there are less sexist examples, too. Many men and women want their partner's approval before buying new food products or garden furniture or a wealth of other things. A lot of teenagers will buy certain products only if their parents *disapprove* of them.

If your customers are likely to be influenced by someone else before buying, you need to know. You can find out through informal and formal research – ask customers whether they take advice from anyone else before making the decision to buy. And if you find out that there is often someone else involved in the decision, make sure you know that 'customer' as well as the one who signs the checks.

Knowledge is the key and the better you know your customers, the smarter you can work. And make sure that you keep learning about them; they will change and their behavior and attitudes will change. So keep up with the developments and you'll be in a prime position to deliver the best service to them a hundred percent of the time.

3

Manage Your Customers

So now you have a solid basis of knowledge about your customers. You have a useful database, packed with information, and you are also keeping up to date with background knowledge about your customers and the world they move in. That's great; but if you're smart, you'll realize that this isn't enough on its own. You have to know how to use all this information.

SMART PEOPLE TO HAVE ON YOUR SIDE:

RICHARD BRANSON

SMART PEOPLE TO HAVE ON YOUR SIDE: RICHARD BRANSON

- Founder of the Virgin Group.
- Believes that the way to achieve satisfied customers is to have satisfied people working on the organization.

Database housework

And before you can even do that, you have to be sure that the information you have continues to be valid. Yeah, yeah, yeah, merging and purging, we know all about that. Well, yes, we all know what merging and purging means, but smart managers also recognize the full importance of the exercise.

For a start, it costs money to mail the same person twice, so the two entries need to be merged. Equally, it's expensive to mail people who no longer exist at the address you have for them, so it makes sense to purge these entries. And for dumb managers that's where the point of the exercise ends.

But hang on a minute. That's only part of the reason for keeping the database clean. The smart approach is to think from the customer's point of view, not simply your own financial perspective. How do your customers feel about duplicate mailings and inaccurate addresses? These questions have actually been researched, at least among business customers, by the Direct Mail Information Service. They discovered that:

- seventy-two percent of business people agreed that duplicate mail 'annoys them intensely'

- seventy-eight percent of business people think that an inaccurate address reflects badly on the company that sent the mailshot.

What's more – and perhaps most worrying of all:

- an average of one in three business mailings contain some form of error in the address.

That should give you some kind of idea of where the dumb approach to merging and purging gets you. You shouldn't be doing it only for your own benefit, but also for your customers. If they are going to feel important and special, they need to feel you've taken the trouble to get your facts right at the very least.

The research results outlined above don't tell you everything; they are just the tip of the iceberg. They do, however, make you wonder about the accuracy of many other database details. How many telephone numbers are wrong on corporate databases around the country? And how many times are customers upset by mailings or phone calls which say, for example, 'As a senior citizen, you might be wondering ...' when they are only 58 years old? Or 'In common with other parents, you will have found ...' when the recipient is not a parent at all, but has been trying desperately for years to have children? At best, you make your customers feel that you know nothing about them; at worst you can deeply upset or offend them.

> *Smart things to say about customers*
>
> You may never achieve a hundred percent accuracy but if you don't aim for it, you won't achieve even ninety percent.

Constant vigilance

Sure, no database is going to be a hundred percent accurate all the time. But be smart, and recognize the importance of accuracy to your relationship with the customer as well as to yourself. Make sure that everyone you work with understands that the database must always be corrected when an inaccuracy comes to light, regardless of how it is discovered. All duplications, out of date details or inaccuracies must be updated as soon as they are identified; not just left for someone else to find when it comes to the annual spring clean.

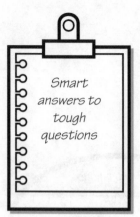
OK, so it wasn't you who entered the wrong data. But you should also ensure that *anyone* who enters details onto the database recognizes the importance of the responsibility. Make sure they always take the time to double-check details, repeat back postcodes and phone numbers to new customers over the phone, and so on. Making new database entries is not a job to be rushed at the expense of accuracy.

And, of course, the database should be spring cleaned regularly. Go through specifically looking for duplications and inaccuracies or incomplete details. You can also send all your customers an annual card – enclosed in a regular mailing – with their details printed on it. Ask them to correct any inaccuracies and return the card to you (you pay the postage). The mere act of asking will make your customers feel you care about them – even the ones who don't need to return the card. Do this regularly so that customers who move should still be getting their mail forwarded when your card arrives.

So you see, taking database cleaning seriously is the first step in managing your customers effectively. While all the dumb managers are dragging down the average number of mailings that have inaccuracies in the address, you can be one of the smart ones who is keeping the average from getting any worse.

Using the database

The database, as we've already established, is not some huge cybermonster which sits at the centre of your organization eating up resources. It is an essential tool for understanding and making the most of your customers. It takes a while to build it up and learn to use it, but once it is established you are bereft without it. Lose it and the whole operation would fall apart. There are two key ways of using the information on your database to get the most from it:

> *Smart things to say about customers*
>
> The database is the corporate Filofax: it contains all the hard facts which you need in order to work effectively.

- using it for analysis

- using it for selection.

Of course these two are interrelated, since a large part of the point of analyzing customer behavior is geared towards deciding how to approach your customers next. But the disciplines are different, so we'll look at them separately.

> *Smart quotes*
>
> 'If you are not in a lifelong learning situation then you are the person who has five years experience in business and one year's experience 35 times.'
>
> *Sir Graham Day*

Analyzing your customers' behavior

If you want to know how customers and prospects will behave in the future, the best guide is to look at how they behave now.

There is an almost endless scope for analysis and the important factor is your skill in working out what you need to know and how to find it out.

The reason supermarkets use loyalty cards is because they tell them so much about their customers' behavior. The vouchers and coupons they hand out to their customers in return for this information are more than paid for by the intrinsic value of the data they collect. Your loyalty card tells them how often you shop with them, how much you spend, which products you buy and so on.

The loyalty card also gives the store the ability to cross reference this information; they can find out whether certain products tend to be bought by the more regular shoppers, whether certain items are bought by customers in particular spending brackets, whether the customers who buy organic wines are the same ones who buy organic vegetables, and so on. And the trick is to know which information to access from their enormous databases, and how to use it profitably.

Your database can be used in exactly the same way. You can combine and cross-reference data to discover whatever you like. Having this amount of information at your fingertips can be a bit scary. Where do you start? Well, there's a simple process:

1. Start by deciding what you need to know.

2. Then find the best way to identify the data you want.

The dumb approach is to wander through your data aimlessly until you find something that looks interesting, or to be so impressed that something is possible that you fail to notice that it is also completely useless.

For example, your database may be able to tell you which of your business customers have an Internet connection at home. If you have the right kind of business to attract customers to a Website outside working hours this could be very useful. But if you sell office stationery to small-ish businesses and the buyer is generally the reception-ist, it's quite hard to see what you could usefully do with this data.

So you need to approach the whole question of data analysis from the right direction. This is probably best illustrated with an example.

Example

Need: We have a new product which our research suggests will ap-peal most to our older customers, particularly those who have reached retirement age. However, we are going to have to price this new prod-uct higher than the rest of our existing range. What we need to know is whether our older customers are likely to buy a more expensive product which suits them particularly well.

Analysis: We need to find out whether our older customers tend to spend more with us than the average, and therefore may be more likely to pay for a more expensive product.

- What is the average spend per order across all our customers?

- What is the average spend per order for our customers over 60?

Your database should give you this information, and it will tell you whether your older customers will be inclined to pay a bit extra. But, if you're smart, you'll have realized that there is still room for doubt. Perhaps your older customers order less often than others. In this case they might not be spending any more overall. By the same token, their average spend per order may appear to be lower than the rest of your customers, but perhaps they order far more frequently. So maybe you should be asking a different set of questions:

- What is the average spend *per year* across all our customers?

- What is the average spend *per year* for our customers over 60?

If you're *really* smart, you will have considered other useful questions to ask as well. If you know your customers through gathering background information about them as we saw in the last Chapter, and understanding what makes them tick, you will know that price may not be the only factor. For example, you may reckon that old people are often more resistant than younger ones to new ideas. Is there a danger that they may reject your new product simply because it's new?

Once again, the answers should be on the database. Just ask it a few more questions:

- What proportion of your customers overall have ordered each of your last five new products?

- What proportion of your customers over 60 have ordered the same products?

- What proportion of each category (overall customers, and customers over 60) ordered the new product within the first year after its launch?

These questions should give you a clue about your older customers resistance or enthusiasm when it comes to new ideas.

The sum of this analysis will give you a far better idea as to whether you should proceed with your new product or whether it seems unpromising. Perhaps you will have to find a way to drop the price before you launch it, or maybe you will need to make it appear less innovative.

This example should demonstrate clearly that while you cannot possibly find out what you need to know about your customers without a good database, neither will you be able to make the most of the information unless you are smart about how you use it. The tool is only as good as the person who is using it; and if you understand your customers and apply your intelligence, you can learn to become an expert in using the database.

Smart quotes

'Grace is given of God, but knowledge is born in the market.'

Arthur Hugh Clough

Selecting target customers

So how do you know which customers to contact? Well, you can select the ones you want to get in touch with using the database. Again, you need to decide who you want to contact before you actually consult your database. You may want to mail all your customers, or prospects, or both. But often you need to select the most appropriate. Clearly the analysis of suitable targets we just

looked at will lead to selection in many cases – in the example above you might end up selecting only those customers over 60, or only those who are both over 60 *and* spend above average with you.

Of course, mailshots aren't the only reason for selecting customers from your database. You might want to produce a list of a particular type of customer for telephone research – such as those who haven't placed an order for over a year, or those who live in a particular region. Or you might want to invite customers from a particular locality to a nearby exhibition you'll be taking a stand at. Perhaps you have a particular product you want to promote to people who work from home, or you have a special offer for companies which do a lot of business with you which you don't want to circulate to other companies.

Analysis and selection generally go hand in hand, and both require an intimate knowledge of your customers and of your database. You need to

SMART PEOPLE
TO HAVE ON
YOUR SIDE:

WILF WALSH

SMART PEOPLE TO HAVE ON YOUR SIDE: WILF WALSH

- Managing director HMV (UK).
- Argues that if a customer perceives a product is faulty, you should assume it is.
- The customer's perception is what matters.

know what information is there, or you won't be able to exploit it. Aim to impress people at meetings by identifying out information your database can provide which they hadn't realized was possible.

Account management

If any term was designed to make a discipline sound boring, it is 'account management'. But in fact, account management makes customers more real, and therefore more interesting. So far, we've looked at managing your customers through the database. This is, of course, an essential basis for customer service, but as an approach it has one flaw: it doesn't focus on customers as individuals, it is a tool for looking at collective behaviors – albeit minority as well as majority behaviors. This is what you need in order to know about your customers, but it is not the best way to know about each customer individually. And although it enables you to give each customer a more personal service than they could hope for without your database, there is a limit to how individual each customer's treatment can really be.

KILLER QUESTIONS

If we want to give our customers the best possible service, shouldn't the most important ones receive a level of service which acknowledges their importance?

When you manage customers through the database, you always start with several thousand – perhaps several hundred thousand – customers. Then you have the option of breaking them down into more manageable groups. This is an ideal approach in many situations, as we've just seen. In particular, it works well for one-off exercises: a specific product launch, a mailshot, a piece of research. But what about the day-to-day servicing of customers?

This is where account management comes in. If your organization has several hundred thousand customers and only a few hundred, or a couple of thousand, employees, you can't possibly have a personal relationship with every single customer. But you can have a personal relationship with the most important ones. You can identify your most important accounts and allocate an account manager to each one. Depending on the size of the customers an account manager may be able to handle anything from one to a hundred accounts.

What's the point of account management?

Account management works particularly well if your organization is one of those for whom a small proportion of customers constitutes a large proportion of your business. These key customers deserve special treatment, and giving it to them will reap rewards. Account managers, along with their teams, can give key customers individual attention. They can offer advice, negotiate customized deals and even develop new services alongside key customers.

As always, there is a dumb way and a smart way to organize this system. Dumb businesses put people in charge of specific customers and then give them no leeway in handling them. They work from a set list of prices, or a sliding scale for bulk sales, and they operate an inflexible system which can't possibly deliver to Birmingham except on a Wednesday, or can't vary its payment terms in any way.

Smart organizations, however, put well trained managers in charge of accounts, equipped with vital skills such as advising, organizing and negotiating. These managers are given the authority to negotiate individual deals with customers, from a position of flexibility where anything goes so long as it fits the conditions which are set – that it must be beneficial for both the organization and the customer. A smart account manager needs to:

- understand both their own business and those of their customers

- advise and influence their customers and their own organization

- plan how they will allocate resources, and how they will improve the relationship with the customer further so as to increase future sales and improve service to the customer

- co-ordinate their own company's departments

- negotiate skilfully with their own organization, their customers and their suppliers.

Well organized account management works extremely well and is extremely profitable. From the customer's point of view, they are getting personal service, with room to manoeuvre and negotiate. They are being treated as important and, crucially, they are getting exactly what they want even if it isn't available to every customer.

From your point of view, you can keep your customers satisfied, you have the flexibility to supply them with whatever they need from you, you are

'When our organization set up a system of account managers, I was made responsible for several customers I had had dealings with before. When they learned that they had been allocated their own account manager, their attitude changed subtly. They adopted a less confrontational style in discussions and negotiations. It was as though they saw me as a sort of friend, and applied social niceties they hadn't when I was just another faceless voice from a supplier's organization.'

in a far better position to use them as a source of information to help you develop new products and services, and you are close enough to spot every opportunity for a sale or a profitable deal with them.

But let's get real. Account management doesn't work in a vacuum. It works only if you have a customer-focused organization. Of course the point of it is that it increases your profits, but it will only do that if you are genuinely serving the customer. Account management simply doesn't bring rewards if you exploit the customer's loyalty and closeness by trying to rip them off or exploit them. They will recognize this kind of behavior far more readily than they would in a more distant relationship.

Account management may not be relevant to all your customers, or even to most of them, but it can bring huge rewards with your most important ones without jeopardizing your relationships with your remaining customers.

What is more, account management is an important step towards relationship marketing, especially on the Internet. It is the forerunner to customer relationship marketing – in other words exploiting the digital technologies of tomorrow to create a personal relationship with every customer.

Who does account management work for?

Account management doesn't work for every organization, but it is an excellent way for many companies to manage their customers. Whether or not your organization uses this approach, it's worth knowing what kind of businesses it is most suited to. That way, you'll be able to see whether your organization is missing out on an important opportunity to improve service to many of its biggest customers, or whether it is trying to apply an account management system where it can't possibly work well.

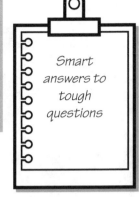
Q: How do we know that setting up an account management system is going to be worth the cost?

A: You might as well ask, how do we know that *not* setting up an account management system will be worth the cost? Failure to operate the most effective system is bound to cost us customers, especially if our competitors are managing their customers effectively.

So here's a rundown of the kind of factors which lend themselves to account management. It works for most organizations, but certainly not for all. It is at its best in organizations where:

- the market is dominated by relatively few big customers; it is less effective if you have a huge customer base of consumers who all give you broadly the same amount of business

- the product or service you are selling is of significance to the customer

- the customer can see a significant difference between your product or service and those of your competitors

- the customer often has a complicated decision-making structure, referring to other buyers with greater authority or better technical knowledge of your product

- there are a lot of opportunities for contact with the customer other than simple order taking, such as advice, maintenance, technical support and so on

- there are good opportunities to create tailored products for the customer, especially when you need close contact to spot the opportunities.

It should also go without saying (except, perhaps, to the dumb managers who may need it spelt out) that if your main competitors manage their customers through key accounts like this, either all of them are wrong or you are.

The pitfalls of account management

Of course, as with any system, there are opportunities to cock it up. There are numerous advantages to managing your customers this way as we have already seen, so long as you focus on the customer and make sure that everything you do benefits them and provides them with excellent service. But that doesn't mean to say that there are no traps for the dumb managers to fall into. It's worth knowing what the major pitfalls are so that you can be sure you don't trip up:

KILLER QUESTIONS

If account management enables you to give better service to your biggest customers without jeopardizing the smaller ones, what reason could there be for not doing it?

- You are more dependent on fewer customers, which obviously makes you a little more vulnerable. Although your other customers are still there, more of your resources are focused on the key accounts. If you lose one of these, or if the customer tries to abuse the flexibility you offer, you are at greater risk.

Smart things to say about customers

If your customer is a professional buyer, make sure they deal with someone equally experienced at your end.

- You generally deal with professional buyers, who are on similar terms with other suppliers and who know exactly how to cut the best deal. This does have its benefits, too, though. Professional buyers understand the system and, while they expect the best possible deal, they recognize that the system has to work for both of you or it will collapse for both of you. If a professional buyer is faced with an untrained novice in your organization, they will most likely tear them to pieces. But if they are dealing with a trained, skilled account manager they will prove to be stimulating and challenging, and also perfectly reasonable.

- There is a risk that your key accounts may benefit at the expense of your rank and file customers. You can avoid this simply by taking it into account when you allocate resources, staff skills and priorities; if you don't, you could be in trouble. Not only is there a danger of losing customers and tarnishing your reputation, but bear in mind that these smaller customers might one day become key customers. So make sure you continue to treat them accordingly.

- Many dumb organizations set up a relationship with a customer and, once it is established, leave it to run itself. This is a complete waste of time and resources. You need to keep working at each account, keep asking what opportunities you could be making more of, and how you could improve your service to the customer. Sometimes, customers fade and are no longer worth giving key account status to; perhaps you can remedy this or perhaps they have changed something about their own operation which means that you couldn't hope to win them back. Equally, some of your rank and file customers may grow to the point where you need to allocate an account manager to them. So make sure that you constantly plan, improve and review your customer relationships.

- It is almost always better to have a team of people working on each account than to have one person solely responsible for each. The danger here is that the relationship can become stale, and one person alone is rarely as creative as a team. It can be stressful coping with an account single-handedly or, at the other end of the scale, it can be easier to run

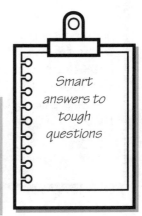

Smart answers to tough questions

Q: Once a key account is up and running, surely the account manager can free up time to set up other accounts?

A: Once the hard work of setting up the account is done, the account manager's time should go into improving the relationship with that customer and the opportunities for more business with them.

out of energy and grind to a halt. The customer can feel lost if their sole contact in your organization moves on and they have to start a brand new relationship. So put together a small team whose members look after a pool of accounts together. The customer will soon get to know them all, and it gives each account continuity if any of the customer's contacts move on. Each team member can help to relieve the others' workload, and a group of people will be more creative when it comes to planning or problem-solving.

Managing customer service

Now here's something really crucial to know about customers: they are constantly measuring the service you provide against the service you said you would provide. And neither of these factors is necessarily what you think it is. For a start, the service the customer perceives that you are providing may not be the same as your perception – they may think it's pretty poor while you think you're doing rather well. And for another thing, you may not think you promised what the customer thinks they heard. Getting both these factors aligned with the customer is what marketing your customer service program is all about.

KILLER QUESTIONS

What's the point of discussing how we think we're doing? It doesn't matter what we think. Isn't the customer's perception the only one that matters?

What sort of service is the customer getting?

We looked at measuring your own performance and your customers' satisfaction levels in Chapter 1. This is critical – and the customer-satisfaction measures are especially critical because you have to know whether they match your own assumptions. To give you an example, suppose your deliveries used to take 28 days from the date of order. You realized that this was far too long, and now you deliver in seven days. You're really pleased with yourselves – you reckon this is great customer service.

But do your customers think so? They'll soon forget what your delivery times used to be, and the new customers won't even know. And anyway, that's not the point. The point is, are they happy to wait seven days for a delivery? Perhaps they want next-day delivery; that makes seven days look pretty poor.

You can, if you're smart, hazard a reasonably good guess as to what they want, so long as you forget your own logistics and just focus on putting yourself in the customer's place. As a customer yourself, if you order a sofa you expect to wait a while; a seven-day delivery time would be excellent. But if you're ordering office stationery, you often need it the next day; seven days would be an unacceptable wait. This kind of intelligent guess can speed up the research process; you know which questions to ask the customer. But you must still check that the customer is satisfied, or you might miss some vital factor which matters deeply to them.

'We sell specialist paint by mail order. I thought about delivery times and figured, nobody decides to start decorating without planning it for a few days, so a three-day delivery time should be fine. But I was wrong. Loads of customers ran out of paint just before the end of the job and wanted another pot the next day so they could finish off. We had to start offering a next-day delivery option to keep them happy.'

SMART VOICES

I thought you thought you heard what I thought I said ...

And what are you offering your customers? You may not ever have said, in so many words, that they can expect a particular level of service from you. But you can raise their expectations subliminally through your advertising, through articles in the trade press, through your mailshots, in your brochures, and in the way your staff talk to them over the phone.

You may not even realize that you are doing this, but your customers will have noticed. If (God forbid) you advertise your product with that hackneyed phrase 'high quality' your customers will assume, for example:

- that it will be easy to assemble/fit/get up and running

- that it will do everything it claims to do without any hassle

- that it will come with a decent guarantee

- that it won't break down anyway – or at least not for years

- that if it did break down, you would sort it out promptly

- that they won't find out after they've bought it that there are loads of better products on the market.

Dumb managers have no idea that they're promising all this, but if you're smart you'll make sure that you are aware of exactly how your customers will interpret your subliminal messages. If your perception and your customers' don't line up, it is often because you've led them to expect something you aren't actually delivering.

> **Smart things to say about customers**
>
> If our perception and the customer's are different, it's us that must change to meet them, not the other way around.

The answer is quite straightforward, in fact. When your customer satisfaction levels drop below what you expect them to be – ask your customers where the problem is. They'll soon let you know where you're going wrong. But better still, don't let it happen in the first place. Think like a customer, and listen to all the implied promises you make. Then make sure that you are offering your customers only what you can deliver.

Marketing customer service

The final piece in this jigsaw is, of course, making sure that what you offer, and what the customer agrees that you are delivering, constitutes excellent service. If you're both agreed that your service is crap and you never promised anything better you have aligned your perceptions but you still haven't achieved one hundred percent satisfied customers. In order to deliver the level of service which your customers both expect and are satisfied with, you need to follow certain guidelines.

> *Smart things to say about customers*
>
> If we can't meet our promises, we should stop making them.

- *Be specific about the service you offer.* The first thing to do is to make sure that all your promises are specific. Don't say that you offer 'great after-sales support', say that you run 'a 24-hour helpline, seven days a week, and that if the problem isn't resolved over the phone we'll send an engineer within four working hours'.

- *Improve the service first, then shout about it.* Many dumb managers who want to improve customer service make the classic mistake of deciding what to do and then telling their customers they're going to do it. Not smart. As soon as you put the idea into the customer's mind, they will expect it now. They won't hear 'We're hoping to offer you ...' they will hear only 'four discounted items a month'. Next month, they want to know what's happened to them.

SMART PEOPLE TO HAVE ON YOUR SIDE: JOSEPH M. JURAN

- Quality guru.
- Helped transform Japanese industry.
- 'Quality planning consists of developing the products and processes required to meet the customers' needs.'

And what if you find you *can't* offer it to them? Or it turns out that it isn't really what they wanted anyway? Maybe they would much prefer a permanent discount on their most frequently ordered item. So improve the service first, make sure it works, confirm through research that customers have noticed and approve of the change, and *then* start to promote it.

- *Consolidate your service promises in writing.* If you make a promise and don't keep it, you're in dead trouble. So you've got to be sure you can meet your undertakings of improved service. And if you can, why not give your promises real clout by putting them in writing, promising concessions if you don't meet them ('If your order hasn't arrived within 48 hours we'll halve the price'), or even building them into the contract.

If you offer concessions they must sound as if they'd hurt you if you want customers to believe in you. If you offer £1 off the repair charge for every day the customer has to wait for an engineer, this isn't very convincing if the cost starts with a £150 call-out fee. If, on the other hand, you waive the entire call-out fee if the customer has to wait over 48 hours, they are much more likely to believe that you'll make the effort to get there within two days.

- *Plan to keep improving your service.* Improving your service gives you a competitive edge in the market. Not only do your customers like the service; they also like the fact that you bothered to improve their lives that little bit. But it won't take the competition long to catch up. Most of the time, if you can do it – they can. So if you've got your repair times down to 48 hours don't rest on your laurels; be smart and start exploring ways to get them down to 36 hours.

- *Keep asking your customers what more they want from you.* Following on from this last point, make sure you are improving the things your customers want improved. If they want repair times down, work on that. But perhaps they don't. Perhaps they don't really mind how long it takes the engineer to arrive, but it's important that the engineer turns up when it suits the customer, and that they can make a reliable appointment accurate within half an hour. Perhaps this is what you should be aiming towards. The customer research we looked at in Chapter 1 is important for giving you just this kind of information.

- *Involve your team.* As a smart manager, you'll know that your team is your front line of customer service, whatever department you run. So you need to make sure their morale and enthusiasm is high so they can transmit this to the customer. But if you keep raising standards, your team is going to have to keep working harder to give more. If you're not careful, morale can drop as a result of constant improvements in customer service, especially if they are unsure whether they can meet your expectations. The team must feel involved in the customer service campaign; they must feel they share in its ownership.

Smart quotes

'Every company should work hard to obsolete its own product line ... before its competitors do.'

Philip Kotler

Smart quotes

'The only irreplaceable capital an organization possesses is the knowledge and ability of its people. The productivity of that capital depends on how effectively people share their competence with those who can use it.'

Andrew Carnegie

SMART PEOPLE
TO HAVE ON
YOUR SIDE:

ANITA RODDICK

For a start, keep your team fully briefed on any planned changes. Invite their ideas and suggestions, and involve them in deciding how best to achieve the changes. Involve them with the customers, too: feature them in advertisements; ask them to talk to customers about how to improve service; make sure customers are given the name of the person they are dealing with; ask the staff to explain the new service levels to customers and explain the reasons for the improvements.

- *Involve your customers.* You also need your customers to be involved in order to make sure that they notice the changes you're making. You can involve them in your advertising; set up focus groups to produce ideas for improving service; ask their advice in problem-solving; invite one or two to training events to talk to your team.

Improving customer service is a constant process, and so is managing and marketing those improvements. It is one of your key weapons in the battle to retain your customers. Your existing customers are far more valuable to you than your prospects who have never yet placed an order, and you must constantly recognize this fact by giving them the service they deserve. In doing so, you will create a reputation and a service which will also draw in your prospects and convert them into new customers.

4

Manage Your Customers' Complaints

Complaints are great; smart managers love complaints. Um ... come again? That's right: complaints are terrific. They are absolutely essential to giving good customer service, and we hope we get lots of them.

OK, well ... in an ideal world we would get no complaints because everyone would be a hundred percent satisfied all of the time. But that's unrealistic. So we'll adopt Plan B: we want people to be totally satisfied as much of the time as possible but, if things do go wrong, we want them to complain.

> *Smart things to say about customers*
>
> Complaints are what give direction to our journey towards total customer satisfaction. Without them, we don't know which areas we need to improve on most.

This is the first point where dumb managers go wrong. They don't like complaints. They don't want them. When they get one, their hearts sink. This is because they are missing the whole point about complaints – complaints are opportunities:

- to identify weak points in the system and put them right

- to make a customer happy

- to create a customer who is more loyal than before.

Yes, a well-handled complaint can leave a customer liking your organization more than if they had never had cause to complain in the first place. This doesn't mean that you should manufacture causes for complaint however, for two reasons. One is that there's always a risk that the customer won't be satisfied with the way the complaint is handled. And the other reason is that if the customer *doesn't* complain, you won't get the opportunity to put things right. And this is the critical point: most unhappy customers don't complain.

The facts about complaints

It's worth knowing a few edifying facts about complaints; unless you understand how and why customers do or don't complain, you can't possibly hope to predict or alter their behavior. Perhaps the scariest fact about complaints is how many customers never tell you when they are unhappy (or should that be 'ex-customers'?):

- For the average business, 96% of unhappy customers don't complain.

Smart answers to tough questions

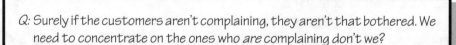

Q: Surely if the customers aren't complaining, they aren't that bothered. We need to concentrate on the ones who *are* complaining don't we?

A: The ones who aren't complaining *are* bothered. They are often so bothered that they leave us without even telling us. The ones who complain are the ones who are at least giving us a chance to hang on to them.

That means that for every complaint you get, there may be 24 customers out there who aren't giving you the chance to put things right, or even to find out what was wrong in the first place. The other contender for the title of 'scariest fact' is this one:

- On average, an unhappy customer will tell between 10 and 16 other people (depending on the seriousness of the complaint) about their bad experience with you. That's double the average number that a satisfied customer will sing your praises to.

Whoops! These statistics show how essential it is to minimize dissatisfaction among customers. But to look on the bright side, such as it is, it is well worth making sure that the complaints you do get are well handled, because:

- When a complainer is satisfied with your response, they will tell only half the number of people about the experience, and they will be positive in the way they talk about it.

KILLER QUESTIONS

However costly it is to set up a proper complaints-handling system, isn't it going to be more costly to keep losing unhappy customers?

What is more, the way you handle the complaint has a huge impact on the likelihood of the customer buying from you again. The available statistics are slightly less specific here, because the figures vary more widely according to the type of industry and the product or service being bought. However, whatever your industry, the principle is clear:

- Up to 90 percent of dissatisfied customers who don't complain will never buy from you again.

- When a customer makes a complaint, and it is dealt with satisfactorily, 35 to 45 percent will still not buy from you again.

- When a customer makes a complaint and it is dealt with quickly and efficiently, however, between 80 and 95 percent *will* continue buying from you.

Losing a customer because they are dissatisfied has all sorts of repercussions. Not only have you lost a customer, but one of your competitors has gained one. There is now, also, someone out there bad-mouthing you whenever your name comes up. If the customer is a business and any of the staff who dealt with you move to another organization which buys from you, there is a danger that this business, too, will be persuaded to abandon you in favor of one of your competitors.

And, of course, look at the revenue you're losing. All those lost orders. How much was that customer spending with you each year? That is the annual number of lost sales for every customer who leaves you because they were dissatisfied. And perhaps you'd like to multiply that figure by 25 to take in all the customers who have stopped buying from you because they were unhappy but never told you so.

Smart things to say about customers

Winning back a dissatisfied customer who has left is considerably harder, and therefore more costly, than winning a completely new customer.

It should now be clear to all but the dumbest managers that only if a customer complains can you increase the likelihood of their remaining a customer, possibly from a ten percent chance of them staying to a 95 per cent chance. So we want customers to complain. Right? We love complaints and we want every dissatisfied customer to complain every time everything isn't a hundred percent how they like it. So the first thing to do is to get those 24 out

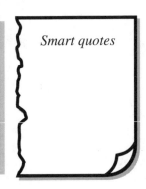
'Those who enter to buy, support me. Those who come to flatter, please me. Those who complain, teach me how I may please others so that more will come. Only those hurt me who are displeased but don't complain. They refuse me permission to correct my errors and thus improve my service.'

Marshall Field

of 25 customers who were unhappy but didn't say so to start saying so, and at least give us a chance.

Encouraging customer complaints

About the smartest thing you can know about customers is that you are one of them. You may not be a customer in your own organization (although of course you may be), but you are certainly a customer hundreds of times over every week in other organizations. So if you want to know how 'customers' behave, think about how *you* behave, and how your family and friends behave. When you are dissatisfied with something you've bought, do you always complain? What determines whether or not you complain?

Answering this question – and thinking about every time you're unhappy as a customer – should help you to understand why your own customers

If I wouldn't settle for this kind of treatment from another organization, how can I justify dishing it out to any of our customers? Can we guarantee that we never treat any of our customers in a way that we would object to if we were the customer?

KILLER QUESTIONS

usually don't bother to complain when they are unhappy. Sometimes it simply doesn't seem worth the effort, but there are often reasons *why* it doesn't seem worth it. Of course, the same reason doesn't apply to every non-complaint, but generally speaking there are three key reasons why customers don't complain:

- they don't know how to

- they think you will be indifferent to them

- they don't like you.

Make it easy to complain

This one often surprises people. Surely it's obvious how to complain, isn't it? You go back to the shop, or pick up the phone, or post a letter, or whatever. But in fact, it isn't always as obvious as it seems. And we all know that sometimes you try to complain to an organization and they tell you that you've come through to the wrong department, or that you'll have to write in. These are dumb organizations, of course, but if you don't let your customers know otherwise, they may assume that you are one of them.

So tell your customers how to complain. Indicate it clearly in your catalogue, put up signs in your shops or reception areas, print it on the packaging, on the invoice and anywhere else you can think of. And remember that customers have different approaches to complaints (think about your own approach); most of us have a preference for phoning, for writing, or for complaining in person. If you insist on written complaints you are not going to encourage those dissatisfied customers who like to use the phone. So give your customers as wide a choice as you can – invite them to phone, write, fax, e-mail or visit one of your offices or retail outlets. Otherwise you not only deter many of them from complaining but you actually wind them up even more.

But don't stop there. A bit of smart thinking should tell you that while all this will help considerably, there is another crucial way of unearthing complaints. It's the approach which solves so many potential problems with customers: ask them. Why wait for them to come to you? If you actively encourage comments, including complaints, your customers will voice far more complaints than they would otherwise. There are several ways of asking your customers what they think:

Smart answers to tough questions

Q: If we actively encourage our customers to complain, aren't we going to be deluged with customers writing, phoning and turning up to make complaints?
A: Yep. Whoopee!

- *Questionnaires.* Send your customers regular questionnaires, such as the customer satisfaction surveys we looked at in Chapter 1, which give them the opportunity to let you know about any problems.

- *Telephone surveys.* You could randomly call a certain number of customers each week to ask if they are happy with the level of service they get from you, or with a recent purchase.

- *Feedback cards.* Hotels most commonly use this method, but it works for a lot of industries. Every hotel room – or every delivery package or new car or train seat or whatever – has a card for the customer to fill in. The quicker this is for them to do, the more likely they are to bother to do it.

- *Carelines.* Advertise a careline number – a freephone number for complaints, advice and enquiries – on every product and invite customers specifically to contact you if they have a problem. Research indicates that simply advertising a careline number can encourage people to buy from you; they feel they will have some recourse if they encounter problems.

- *Video-points*. Some organizations put up booths rather like passport photo booths where customers can sit and make a video of themselves telling you what they think of you, good or bad.

Let them know it's worth it

Of course, if you're going to get your customers to tell you how they feel, you must be prepared to respond to them. Customers simply aren't going to bother filling in a questionnaire or phoning a careline if you're not going to do anything about it.

> **Smart things to say about customers**
>
> One of the chief factors which deters many people from complaining is that they don't believe it will have any effect.

Make any offers you can in writing in catalogues, on signs or on delivery documentation. If you can guarantee a no-quibble replacement or money back, say so. The more a customer believes that their complaint will benefit them, the more likely they are to make it. Word of mouth is important, too; customers will tell colleagues or friends if complaining was worthwhile, and those colleagues and friends will be more (or less) likely to bother complaining in the future. Similarly, if a customer has ever complained to you before, their own past experience will give them a big clue as to whether it's worth the effort of complaining this time round.

When you encourage dissatisfied customers to respond to questionnaires, feedback cards and so on, you must have a system for dealing with all complaints effectively when you receive them. We'll look at complaint-handling systems in a moment, but the point is that if you invite a customer to complain and then don't respond, you've done more damage than if you never asked them in the first place. It's like inviting a friend round and then being out for the evening when they turn up.

As soon as you ask a customer to complain, you raise their expectation that it will be worth their while doing so. If it isn't, the gap between their expectation and the reality is greater than it would have been if you'd printed a note on the invoice which said 'If you're not happy, don't bother to complain; we're not interested.' At least then you would have delivered exactly what they expected.

So your response must be effective, in every way. Complaints made on questionnaires and feedback cards must be followed up swiftly; carelines must be answered promptly, and by a real person not an answering machine; complaints unearthed during telephone surveys must be dealt with – at least initially – by the person making the survey call.

Be likeable

Here's something which may strike a chord with you when it comes to your own decisions about whether or not to make complaints. People are more likely to complain to an organization they like than to one they don't. How often have you done this yourself? If you like an organization, you want to give them the benefit of the doubt. You want to go on liking them, so you give them a chance to let you. Just as you give good friends a second chance if they let you down, so you give friendly companies another stab at getting it right and restoring your faith in them. Apart from anything else, it justifies your original view of them. If you don't complain, and don't buy from them again, you are in a sense admitting that *you* were wrong to like them in the first place.

Think about the reverse of this. If you don't like an organization, you are much less likely to complain. You think 'Sod them. Why should I give them my business anyway? And why should I give them the satisfaction of telling them where they went wrong?' You may not have got any recompense for whatever the problem you encountered was, but at least you have the quiet satisfaction of knowing that you've lost them custom *and* you have given them no clues to help them avoid repeating their mistake with the next customer. *And* you're going to make sure you tell everybody you can never to do business with them ever again. So there.

Being likeable buys you chances. Your customers will be far more indulgent with you. Of course it's hard to be likeable if you keep messing up, but we all make some mistakes, and likeable companies get away with them far more often. Popular organizations like the Virgin Group or the Body Shop get forgiven far more frequently than unpopular ones such as the local electricity board.

What makes companies likeable? We're into the whole enormous question of corporate image and branding here, which could (and does) fill several books. But actually, despite the fact that there are numerous books out there on the subject, many of them excellent, there are only really two things that make an organization likeable:

- its people

- its customer service.

And of course, even these two factors are closely related.

Customers judge an organization by the people within it who they deal with. If everyone they talk to is helpful, they see the company as a helpful organization. If everyone is obstructive, they think the organization is obstructive. It's quite simple. So your job is to make sure that everyone in your team always behaves in the most likeable way possible when they deal with customers: always friendly, helpful, efficient and so on. Just one contact where the standard slips can result in a customer whose view of the organization is not what it should be; and that one customer becomes a potential non-complainer, a potential go-and-see-if-the-competition-treat-me-any-better ex-customer.

Likeable staff is the most important factor in being a likeable organization. But it has to be backed up by likeable systems. Suppose the staff are always friendly and helpful and offer you an immediate replacement for your faulty product, but the replacement takes three weeks to turn up, and then it's the wrong item, and then you sort it out on the phone with the friendly, helpful staff but the computer invoices you anyway ... There comes a point where you stop forgiving even the most likeable staff.

> *Smart things to say about customers*
>
> Our systems must work with our own people, not against them. Giving our customers messages which conflict cannot have the same impact as giving them messages which reinforce each other.

So it's vital that the systems are as helpful and effective as the staff, and geared to what the customer wants. If you have likeable people and likeable systems, it is extremely difficult to stop your customers liking you.

It's worth adding one rider to this, however. It can take a very long time – and I mean several years – for your customers to notice that you're likeable if you haven't always been. Attitudes change very slowly and, if your customers don't particularly like you, it can take them years to notice – and then to believe – that you have changed your ways.

Remember that improving your image and your levels of customer service may occupy most of your working hours. To your customers, however, you are just one of hundreds of suppliers they deal with from time to time, and between those times they barely even remember that you exist. How much time do you devote to thinking about your local dry cleaners when you're not actually in the shop? And if they suddenly launched a drive to be friendlier to customers, how long would it take you to notice – honestly?

Making complaints self-reducing

When you first start to encourage complaints actively, the aim should be for the level of complaints you receive to rise. You want it to rise enormously. This is pretty nerve-racking of course, and you need to be ready for it. What is more, if you're responsible for the campaign to encourage complaints – in the whole organization or just in your own part of it – you'll need to warn senior management to expect a jump in the number of complaints. To the dumber members of your organization, this may not seem logical. But to the smart thinkers, it is a dream come true.

The point is that you are not increasing the number of dissatisfied customers at all. You're simply persuading the non-complainers to become complainers. The average organization can, in theory, increase complaints by up to 25 times without creating a single additional unhappy customer. All you're creating is opportunities to turn unhappy customers into happy

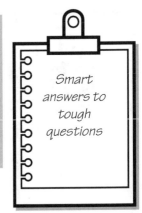

> Q: Surely encouraging more customers to complain means encouraging the dissatisfied customers to focus on their dissatisfaction rather than forget about it?
>
> A: But they won't forget about it anyway. Sure, they might ignore it for the moment, but next time we cock up, or next time a competitor approaches them, they will still be bearing a grudge – one which we haven't had the opportunity to resolve.

ones. So it isn't simply that you don't *mind* getting more complaints; it is a case of cracking open the champagne when it happens.

If you find this idea rather frightening, which most people understandably do, there is a way of reassuring yourself about it. Look at your customer satisfaction ratings (this is yet another reason for regularly measuring customer satisfaction). Despite getting more complaints, satisfaction levels shouldn't drop. In fact, you may well find that they rise as customers like to feel that complaining, should they want to do it, will be simple, straightforward and effective.

Using your complaints

In the long term, of course, you want complaints to reduce because you want the number of dissatisfied customers to reduce continually. After the initial jump in complaints, numbers should fall off as rapidly as possible. And the way to make this happen is simple: listen to the complaints. Don't simply resolve each one ad hoc, but use the information the complaints give you to remove the causes of complaint.

To give you an example, Polaroid in the US set up a customer careline. By analyzing the reasons for the calls they received, they discovered that one of the most common customer complaints was that they didn't include batteries in their film packs. By doing so, they could slash the number of dissatisfied customers (the important thing) and the number of complaints (the next most important thing).

If you record the complaints which come in, you'll find out where the scope for improving customer service is. And each time you address one of these areas, you can have a dramatic effect on customer satisfaction levels and on complaints. So when you start to listen to your complaints and act on them, the level of complaints should not reduce gradually but in large jumps, especially at first. You should be able to wipe out huge numbers of potential future complaints at a time by responding effectively to the complaints you receive.

So the pattern when you launch a drive to encourage customers to complain should be:

- actively encourage complaints in as many ways as possible

- measure your success by the jump in the number of complaints

- check against customer satisfaction ratings that the complaints have increased but dissatisfaction hasn't

- listen to the complaints and analyze them

- *act on the complaints*

- watch complaint levels drop back.

Who deals with complaints?

In some organizations, complaints are handled by a complaints department (it may be called a 'customer service' department, but we all know it's a complaints department really). Sometimes the manager of the department responsible deals with the complaint. And sometimes the person responsible for the problem (whether or not it was actually their fault) deals with it.

But there is a better option than all of these, and the smart thinking manager will realize exactly what it is: if the customer directs a complaint at a particular person, simply let that person handle the complaint. Let's go back to thinking of yourself as the customer. When you complain to an organization, who do you want your complaint handled by? Usually the answer is the first person you speak to. If you write, you want it dealt with by the person to whom you addressed the letter, fax or e-mail – presumably that's why you addressed it to them.

KILLER QUESTIONS

Why can't the customer choose who deals with their complaint?

The customer usually doesn't give a damn what the job title or department is of the person they are speaking to. All they are interested in is getting their complaint resolved as swiftly as possible. And the fastest way to do that is if the person they first speak to sorts the problem out for them. Of course, some serious complaints need to be dealt with by someone with more authority, but you should make sure that your front-line staff have as much authority as possible to handle complaints.

Dumb managers tend to think that their team members are dumb too, and treat them accordingly. They daren't allow them to handle complaints in case they get it wrong, so they insist that all complaints are passed on to them or to the relevant department. This serves to confirm their dumbness of course: by refusing to deal with the complaint at the first point of contact they are guaranteed to irritate their dissatisfied customer further.

Customers aren't stupid (even dumb managers can be quite smart on days off when they become customers). Your customer knows that the receptionist isn't likely to be able to give them a free two-week holiday in the Seychelles to compensate them for the one they just took where they were put in a dirty hotel three miles from the beach. Of course that level of compensation will need to be authorized by someone further up the organization.

But if the customer simply wants a replacement for a faulty alarm clock they've just bought, it's hard to see why the shop assistant can't give it to them. Most importantly, the customer can't see why not, so insisting on referring the complaint is simply going to make them even more annoyed than they are already – and even less likely to do business with your organization again.

Smart answers to tough questions

Q: How can we let front-line staff take responsibility for handling complaints when they don't know how to do it properly?
A: Because our customers want it that way. Our responsibility is to make sure our front-line staff *do* know how to handle complaints by training them in the techniques and explaining the benefits to both them and the customer.

Giving front-line staff the authority to deal with complaints themselves is far better for their morale. As well as feeling trusted with the responsibility, it makes complaints easier to take. When faced with an irate customer, instead of being obliged to make them even angrier by not giving them what they want, they are in a position to satisfy them – a much easier and more rewarding encounter to have.

There is another factor which is important here, as well. The cost of passing complaints up the line can be enormous, when you take into account staff time:

- Research shows that a complaint review by senior staff can cost up to 15 times as much as handling the complaint informally at the front line.

- Apart from that, the longer the complaint takes to resolve, the more it will take to satisfy the customer. You can end up having to give them a full refund where they might well have settled for a replacement or even just an apology when they first made the complaint.

- What is more, if the complaint is not dealt with quickly, you are much more likely to lose the customer permanently, so you should also calculate in the lost revenue.

It should be clear that complaints should always be handled by the person the customer first approaches.

What if the complaint is so serious that it must be passed up the organization? Or so technical that it can only be dealt with by a particular department? Well, obviously if it has to be, it has to be. But the person who first receives the complaint should still take responsibility for it until it is passed on:

- They should make sure that the customer understands why it is in their own interest to have their complaint referred.

- They should make sure they pass the complaint direct to the best person, so the customer doesn't have to go through a series of people to find the right one.

- they should follow the complaint until it has been fully handed over; it's no good leaving a message for someone to call the customer back and then forgetting about it. They should make sure the message gets through, and not relinquish responsibility until they have established that the call-back to the customer has been made.

Dear sir or madam ...

Suppose a customer writes to you personally with a complaint. Or to the MD. Or to any other manager in the organization for that matter. If a customer chooses to write to a member of management it is because they consider their complaint to be serious enough to warrant being dealt with by someone senior. Don't offend them by passing their complaint down the line. If you've ever written a letter of complaint to an MD and received a reply from the customer services manager you'll know how it feels. There are sometimes difficulties with this approach, but there are also ways around them, so long as you stay focused on the customer and what will satisfy them:

- The customer will not generally mind if the reply comes from someone equally senior to you – and they certainly won't mind a reply from someone more senior – if there's a good reason which is made clear. So you can pass a complaint over to a manager better equipped to deal with it, but you should still make sure it is dealt with satisfactorily.

- You should have time to deal with this kind of complaint yourself. Even if you are the MD, what could you be spending your time on which is more important than keeping your customers happy? But sometimes it really isn't possible to respond quickly yourself. In this case, delegate the job of researching and writing the response, but still read the letter and sign it yourself. Don't get someone else to *pp* it.

- If you're away, and someone else deals with the letter, write to the customer on your return. Explain that you've been away, have just seen their letter, understand their complaint has been resolved, but are writing to make sure they are now happy (and maybe reiterate an apology or whatever).

- Sometimes, the best person to deal with the complaint is less senior than you. There are two options here. Either get the information you need from them and then reply to the customer yourself, or pass the letter on but write to the customer yourself as well. This lets them know that it isn't that their complaint is beneath you, it's just that your colleague should be more useful to them. Let them know in the letter that if they are not completely satisfied you want them to come back to you personally and let you know.

Handling complaints effectively

OK, so we know who is going to handle the complaint. But how will they handle it? As always, they should handle it the way the customer wants them to. So what way is that? We need to know what it is that matters to customers when it comes to handling complaints, and the top factor is absolutely clear in surveys which have been conducted among consumers. The single most important factor in resolving a complaint is:

Speed

The customer doesn't want any more of their life than necessary taken up with this complaint. It's bad enough that the product or service wasn't satisfactory in the first place, without you wasting their time putting it right. This is a key reason for training front-line staff to deal with as many complaints as possible – it's faster.

One research project within one particular company surveyed the satisfaction levels of customers who had complained. When complaints had taken less than four hours to resolve, the final number of satisfied customers was more than double what it was when complaints took *more* than four hours to resolve. The point here is clear, although the timings will depend on the business you're in. If you've taken a faulty alarm clock back to the shop, you probably expect it to be sorted out on the spot. If you're complaining to a travel agent about a serious problem with the holiday you've just

Smart things to say about customers

It doesn't matter what *we* think is a fast time for resolving a complaint. What counts is whether the customer thinks we have resolved it quickly. When assessing the speed of our response to complaints, we must always judge from the customers' perspective, not our own.

returned from, you may expect it to take a few days. But whatever your industry, the faster you resolve the problem, the more customers you will satisfy.

Don't forget to include the length of time it takes the customer to contact you in the first place. You must have phoned organizations yourself who you simply can't get through to on the phone. If you have a complaint which you can't even register because the damn company won't pick up the phone, what does it do to your blood pressure? Just make sure that your customers aren't having this problem with you.

There's another important factor, too, which is often related to speed but isn't the same thing. How many times does the customer have to contact you before their problem is resolved? Once the customer has contacted you with the complaint, you should make sure that every subsequent contact is initiated by you. That means you have to reply to their letter, keep them informed on the phone, or whatever it takes, before they decide to contact you to chase up their complaint. If you aren't convinced of the importance of this, have a look at another scary set of statistics:

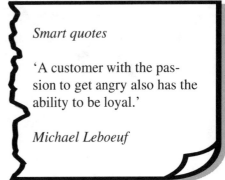

Smart quotes

'A customer with the passion to get angry also has the ability to be loyal.'

Michael Leboeuf

- if a complaint is resolved with only one contact, just over 50 percent of customers (on average) will remain loyal

- if the customer has to contact you only twice, the percentage of loyal customers plummets to just over 30 percent

- if it takes three or more contacts to get you to sort the problem out, the percentage nose-dives to just 16 percent.

So make sure that the customer never has to pick up the phone or the pen, or come back into the shop, after their first contact.

The next most critical factor quoted by customers is:

Being kept informed

Tell them what is happening about their complaint. Contact them frequently to reassure them that it is being dealt with and let them know what is going on. Keeping customers informed actually buys you time. Customers are more satisfied if you keep them posted while you're resolving their complaint than if you don't, *even if it takes longer to resolve it.*

> **Smart things to say about customers**
>
> If you're not sure how often to contact the customer, ask them. But if in doubt, contact them anyway. It's difficult to give a customer too much information about the progress of their complaint.

Obviously there are limits here, and the customer would still rather have the speed *and* the information, but keeping them informed is vital. And if there is no progress for some reason? You should still contact them and let them know that you still haven't been able to contact the technical manager, or find the missing order form, or whatever, but you'll get back to them again shortly.

Here is a list, in descending order, of the factors which customers quoted as being the most important in handling their complaints:

1. speed

2. being kept informed

3. having a fair investigation

4. having a clear procedure

5. friendliness and helpfulness

6. dealing with a named person.

What's the point of complaining?

If you're going to understand customers, you have to understand *why* they complain. What do they hope to achieve? Well, the simplest way to find out is to ask them. Often, in fact, they let you know very clearly: 'I demand my money back!' or 'I want this replaced at once.' If not, you can simply ask them: 'What can I do to resolve this for you?' If the customer is in a good temper, more often than not you should be able to give them what they ask for. If they are irate, they will frequently demand far more than they expect – it's a kind of challenge to you. They'll ask for a complete free replacement holiday just because the food at the hotel they stayed at wasn't up to scratch. With good handling (which we'll look at in a moment) they should drop their demands to something more reasonable.

Smart quotes

- 'Rule #1: The customer is always right.

- 'Rule #2: If you find the customer is wrong then return immediately to Rule#1.'

Stew Leonard

Sometimes, customers aren't clear what they want. Perhaps they only really wanted to let off steam, but feel they deserve some kind of compensation. In this case an excellent approach is to offer them a choice. 'We can replace this item for you, or we could give you a full refund if you prefer.'

The psychology behind this approach is important. Many customers feel under-confident about complaining. Perhaps they think you'll just tell them to sod off and they won't know what to do next. Perhaps they were brought up always to be polite and find it difficult to complain. Maybe they think you'll tell them that your product is fine, and it's their fault it has broken.

Customers who get irate are often worried they won't be believed – they get angry because they think that attack is the best form of defence, and they are on the defensive before they pick up the phone or walk into the store. The more likely they think you are to believe them, the less likely they are to get angry.

Whatever the reason, complainers often feel that you are in control of the encounter, and they are at your mercy.

So the best way to pacify and satisfy a complaining customer is to let them see that they are in control of the conversation, not you. And letting them choose how the complaint is resolved is one of the best ways of doing this. You're inviting them to give you your instructions. Of course, you've only offered them the choice which suits you, but that doesn't matter. It's a psychological game and the offer you make is a coded way of letting them know that they are the important one.

Although every complaint is individual – and should be treated as such – there are certain things which customers tend to want as a result of complaining. It is quite useful, especially if you're planning an overhaul of your department or organization's complaint-handling system, to know what customers most often hope to gain by complaining. So here is a list, in descending order, of the reasons for complaining among customers surveyed:

- to get better service

- to get money or a service they are eligible for

- to get an explanation

- to prevent the same thing happening to others

- to get an apology

- 'to tell them what I thought of them'

- to get compensation

- to vent anger or frustration.

It's interesting to note how many of these reasons for complaining do not require any recompense of material value from you. The customer frequently wants reassurance, wants to be taken seriously, wants to be treated as important, wants to be listened to, wants to be given an explanation. It should be clear that if you have really good customer service, and always let your customers know that they are important, that you listen to them, and so on, you will generate far fewer complaints.

Not just satisfaction, but excellence

We saw at the beginning of the chapter that the difference between dealing with a complaint satisfactorily and dealing with it really well can have a huge impact on whether the customer buys from you again. So how should you and your team, and the rest of the organization, deal with complaints when you receive them? There are plenty of books and training materials

SMART PEOPLE
TO HAVE ON
YOUR SIDE:

JAMES DYSON

SMART PEOPLE TO HAVE ON YOUR SIDE: JAMES DYSON

- Founder of Dyson Appliances.
- Invented the bagless dual cyclone vacuum cleaner as a result of being a dissatisfied customer of a traditional vacuum-cleaner company.

on the subject so we won't go into detail, but let's just check out the principles of good complaint handling.

There are two factors here, both of which we've touched on already: the psychology of complaint handling and the practicalities.

Psychology

- Be friendly, pleasant and helpful even if you're confronted by anger or rudeness.

- Make it clear to the customer that both they, and their complaint, are important to you. Take them seriously.

- Listen to their side of the story – they may need to let off steam.

- Sympathize with them. This doesn't mean admitting responsibility; if they tell you that the new video player broke down just as their grandchild was sitting down to watch their favorite tape you can simply say 'Oh, no. How upsetting.' You've admitted nothing, but you've indicated that you acknowledge their feelings.

- By the same token, don't start trying to justify your actions, or those of your colleagues or organization. It's not important. Focus on the customer's need to resolve the problem.

- Never argue with the customer. If they are the one who is important, that means you aren't important just at the moment. Nor are your views. The customer doesn't want to know *why* the video player doesn't work, they just want it fixed.

KILLER QUESTIONS

If the customer's perception of the situation is what matters, why can't we just assume that every customer complaint is justified without having to check it?

Practicalities

- Your priority is to solve the problem in a way which satisfies the customer. So find out what they want – and do it, as quickly as possible.

- Keep the customer regularly informed as to what is happening.

- If it really isn't possible, explain why to the customer and offer them an alternative. If the explanation is reasonable, the customer (now you've shown them they are important) will accept it. If it is unreasonable, why are you giving it?

- Make sure that the customer is happy with the solution you've arrived at together; if they are not, it isn't a solution. It's no good trying to foist a solution onto a customer; they won't end up satisfied.

- Finally, follow it up and make sure it happens: check the engineer actually turns up, or the accounts department rectifies the invoice, or a replacement item is sent out promptly.

There are two things to add to this, both of which we have touched on earlier in the book. First of all, here's another reason why it's so smart to have a good database. If you're dealing with a complaint over the phone or by letter, fax or e-mail, you should be able to call up the customer's details on the database. This means you can check their history with you: have they been a customer for long? Have they had cause to complain before? How often? Have they ever had to complain about the same problem before? If they rang you only last month about an incorrect statement, and now you've sent them another one, you really should know about it when you speak to them.

> **Smart things to say about customers**
>
> If we can refer back to our shared history with the customer when they make a complaint, the customer will feel far more important because we've bothered to find out all about them.

The other point worth making here is one we made in Chapter One about giving one hundred percent service. Always look for ways to give the customer that little bit more than they asked for. Don't just sort out the incorrect statement; give them a five percent discount this month. Don't just replace the faulty video player; give them a pack of free video tapes to go with it. Give the customer what they want to satisfy them – and then give them something more. This is the kind of thing which ensures customers keep coming back. Their attitude should be 'Well, everyone makes mistakes. But at least with this lot you know they'll sort them out quickly and efficiently.'

The complaints system

We've looked at the best approach to individual complaints to ensure the maximum number of satisfied customers. But you also have to operate a proper system of collating and analyzing these complaints in order to make sure that you act to prevent them recurring, as we saw earlier.

There are plenty of different ways of organizing the details of such a system, but they all have certain features in common to enable the organization to benefit fully from the complaints it receives. So here's a guide to the key features on an effective complaints handling system.

Define a 'complaint'. If everyone is going to be trained to handle complaints and be involved in the complaints-handling system – and we have established by now that they should be – there needs to be a consensus on what constitutes a complaint. Otherwise one person will be logging every contact with a customer who politely points out an error while another will record only those occasions when the customer gets really annoyed, or will omit to record those occasions when they reckon the problem was the customer's fault anyway.

Generally speaking, you should regard as a complaint every expression of less than one hundred percent satisfaction by a customer, even if it is expressed pleasantly and without irritation. Suppose a customer rings up to 'query an invoice'. It turns out there is an error, and you assure them it will be rectified on the statement at the end of the month. They are quite happy with this and thank you politely for checking it out. But however happy they seem, they would surely have preferred an accurate invoice in the first place. This would have saved them a phone call to you if nothing else.

There are, however, a few industries where the definition needs to be a little different. Take BT as an example. They do not define every report of a fault as a complaint, since they expect faults on telephone lines from time to time, and so do their customers, and these are recorded and analyzed anyway. They do, however, count a fault report as a complaint if the customer gives any indication of dissatisfaction, even in the tone of their voice. You could argue that even if faults are expected they still leave customers less than one hundred percent satisfied; the point is debatable. What is important, however, is that everyone at BT is clear about how they actually define complaints, and every department is logging them on the same basis.

> *Smart quotes*
>
> 'A problem is a chance for you to do your best.'
>
> *Duke Ellington*

Log every complaint. All complaints should be logged by the person who receives and handles the complaint. You may do this on your database or you may do it on paper. Either way, you should record all the information you need, but still aim to keep the process as brief as possible so that people always have time to fill in the log. It is your job to make sure that everyone on your team understands that it is well worth the time it takes and the log must be completed fully. Here's a guide to the data you need to record; you can produce a complaint form on a single side of paper asking for this information:

- name, address, phone number of customer

- name of person who handled the complaint

- date of complaint

- nature of complaint

- action to be taken

- customer's response to the solution agreed

- when will the action be taken?

- who is responsible for taking it?

- any suggestions to prevent the problem recurring.

Record and analyze all complaints centrally. All complaint forms should be sent to a single department which is responsible for classifying them and analyzing them. This should bring to light any recurring weak spots or frequent areas of complaint. You can look for particular themes or note whether complaints are more common at particular times or with particular product lines.

SMART PEOPLE TO HAVE ON YOUR SIDE: SAM WALTON

- Founder of Wal-Mart retail chain.
- Believed in the superlative importance of great customer service: 'Our goal as a company is to have customer service that is not just the best, but legendary.'

Feed back the analysis. This information should be fed back to the departments so that they can develop strategies and solutions to resolve the causes of complaint and minimize future complaints. These strategies should be fed back to the central department so that they can take them into account in future analyses, and see how effective they have been.

Inform senior management. Regular reports on complaints analysis, and the strategies developed to counter the complaints, should be passed to senior management. Smart senior managers will want to review these regularly, along with customer satisfaction ratings. Smart directors will expect reports on both complaints and customer satisfaction ratings to be submitted in time for every board meeting.

5

Build Customer Loyalty

Once you have a good base of customers, your most important aim should be to hold on to them. The dumb approach – adopted all too often – is to think that once you have won a customer you can stop worrying about them and move on to recruiting more customers. But customers don't necessarily stay with the same suppliers; they can leave you for your competitors any time. And they often do.

- It costs between three and seven times as much to win a new customer as it does to hang on to an existing one.

> **Smart quotes**
>
> 'Treat the customer as an appreciating asset.'
>
> *Tom Peters*

This statistic alone should make it clear why it is such a smart move to concentrate on your existing customers. It is vital that you keep the customers you have and, only once you have mastered that skill, should you start to build your customer base with new contacts.

Customers are people. They may seem to be faceless ones; they may even seem to be other businesses and not people at all. But it is people – individuals – who decide whether or not they or their business will buy from you. And people have certain personality traits which are pretty universal:

KILLER QUESTIONS

How can we justify putting any resources into recruiting new customers until our customer turnover reaches virtually nil?

- they want to be liked

- they want to be treated with the respect and importance they deserve

- they want attention

- they want their behavior to be recognized and appreciated

- they want to communicate with other people whom they like.

Just because they are customers and you are a supplier, doesn't mean that any of these basic human wants have changed. You need to bear all these factors in mind when dealing with customers, just as you do with your own partner in a relationship. Look through the bullet points again; if you ignored all of these when dealing with a partner, you could hardly be surprised if in the end they went off with someone else. You'd do the same to them. And as a customer, you'd do the same to your suppliers.

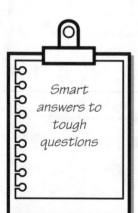

Smart answers to tough questions

Q: If customers are so demanding, how can anyone hope to keep them satisfied?
A: The harder it is to keep customers happy, the more of a competitive edge we will have if we are the ones who manage to do it.

Why do customers leave you?

You might be interested to know what it is that persuades customers to leave. One survey asked customers exactly this question, and the results are worth reading:

The customer moved	3%
They developed a good relationship with another supplier	5%
They found a cheaper product elsewhere	9%
They were unhappy with the product or service	15%
They left due to lack of contact, indifference or the attitude of the supplier	68%

In other words, over two-thirds of customers who leave do so because of your attitude to them. It actually takes quite a substantial price difference between you and your competitors to persuade a customer to leave you for a cheaper supplier. This shouldn't be a great surprise, since your prices probably haven't changed that much relative to your competitors since the customer decided to start buying from you.

Fifteen percent of customers who leave do so because they are unhappy with your products or services. The smart moves we've looked at in the first half of this book should help to reduce that figure out of all recognition. If you implement an effective customer service program, unearth complaints and then deal with them,

KILLER QUESTIONS

If our customers knew when they started buying from us that we weren't the cheapest on the market, why on earth should that knowledge stop them buying from us now?

you should be able to slash the number of customers who leave because of poor products or unsatisfied complaints.

What about the customers who leave because they develop a good relationship with another supplier? Well, that may be the reason they give in the survey, but what they actually mean must be more specific. They must mean that the relationship with the other supplier is good *and* better than their relationship with you. In other words, you've still left scope for improvement, and one of your competitors has filled that scope. If your attitude to your customers were faultless, they would not have been likely to move. In other words, it's your own fault.

Remember that, for a customer, it's often really quite a hassle to change suppliers. There's always a level of risk in changing, too; the new supplier might turn out to be no better than the last. Meantime they've had to devote effort to researching and choosing alternative suppliers and perhaps reviewing the whole buying procedure. So if there's no difference between the present supplier and a new one, the customer will almost invariably choose to stay with the one they are already with.

> *Smart things to say about customers*
>
> For a competitor to win a customer from you, you must have been failing the customer in some way.

What goes wrong?

Your customers were happy to buy from you initially, and often continue to do so for some time before they start to look around for another supplier. So presumably your level of service to them was fine to start with and has declined some time since – at least in their eyes. So where did you go wrong?

Just as with a new love affair, we tend to start by wooing our customers. We give them lots of attention, make appealing offers to them, perhaps even give them gifts. We make them feel wanted and special. But once we have won them, we are at risk of beginning to take them for granted. We tend to neglect them in favor of a newer challenge. Pursuing new interests can start to seem more important.

- We might stop visiting our existing customers and simply phone them instead.

- Perhaps we put our resources into creating offers and special deals for the next new customer instead of for the existing one.

- Returning phone calls to existing customers can move down the priority list; it may take us a day or two to reply to a phone call.

- Likewise it may seem a low priority to chase up queries, put together quotes or even deal with complaints for 'old' customers.

- Perhaps we are more reluctant to customize products or services, or make one-off arrangements, with existing customers.

- Maybe we stop asking the customer questions – either because we assume we know the answers or because we've lost interest. We no longer check that they are happy with the product (well, they'd say if they weren't, wouldn't they?). We don't ask them about their own market, and how we fit in with their objectives for the future.

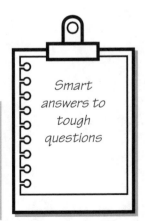

Smart answers to tough questions

Q: How are we supposed to notice when our attitude to our customers changes?
A: If we have to ask the question about any customer, our attitude has already changed. If we don't actively notice and recognize our customers, we are taking them for granted.

If the relationship was good to begin with, we might be forgiven for the first few lapses of attention. And for a while, our customers may put up with our new behavior because it's less hassle than looking around for another supplier, and anyway if we changed once, maybe we can change back. But sooner or later the relationship will disintegrate too far. All it takes is for one of our competitors to come along with gifts and offers and attention, and the customer will desert us.

Keeping up the momentum

So the trick is to keep the relationship fresh. Continue to treat each customer in the way we did when we first started to woo them. Remember that the customer needs an incentive to remain loyal to us. The deeper their loyalty to us goes, the harder it will be for a competitor to prise them away from us. And the way to encourage and develop that loyalty is to remember that customers are people.

Like your customers

Be honest – do you actually like your customers? You must have been dealt with at some time by a business supplier, a shopkeeper, a ticket inspector or some other supplier in a way which suggested that they disapproved of you or your standards. Perhaps they look down their noses at you because your choice of sofa indicates such dreadful taste, or clearly can't be bothered with you because your order is so small. It has happened to all of us. And the mere fact that the supplier doesn't like or approve of us is sufficient to put us off the organization. As we've seen before, each person who deals with a customer represents the organization to that customer. The fact that the other shop assistant might have thoroughly approved of your taste in sofas counts for nothing; if the one who serves you dislikes your taste then, as far as you're concerned, the whole organization dislikes your taste.

Quite why some people behave like this can be puzzling. It's hard to see how they think it can help their customer relations to demonstrate dislike or disapproval for their customers. The reason is generally that the shop assistants (or receptionists or accounts staff or maintenance engineers or whoever) get their pay packet at the end of the week regardless of whether that customer comes back or not. They are happy to demonstrate their superior taste or judgement or behavior (as they see it) at the expense of losing customers, because it's not their problem.

The answer, clearly, is to demonstrate to everyone in the organization that it *is* their problem. Your own staff, from top to bottom of the company, must understand that it is essential to like the customers and to show it. As with the whole customer service program, you must train everyone to recognize its importance and to see that customers must be popular and must realize that they are liked.

Culture shift

In many organizations, this can call for a shift in culture. It is often endemic in organizations to criticize customers behind their back, to send them up, and to pretend to obstruct and irritate them – in some organizations it is even the practice to obstruct customers for real. Some organizations have whole departments which take pleasure in sending out orders late to difficult customers, or processing the order incorrectly to 'punish them' for being rude. It is hardly surprising these customers are rude and difficult.

This attitude – even in its milder forms – makes it extremely difficult for staff to like and respect the customers. The peer-group pressure to dismiss or look down on customers can be so strong that no one wants to be the first to admit that actually some of the customers are OK really. It is imperative that you change this culture, starting in your own team – even at the expense of being seen as a sanctimonious party pooper. You don't have to deny that some customers are more demanding than others, but you do need to make it clear that gratuitous negativity towards customers just isn't acceptable.

We are all very susceptible to believing our own words. Even though we think we know that we don't really dislike the customers, 'we were just saying it', our view of customers is colored over time by this attitude. It is very hard to like someone when you always discuss them as though you didn't like them. So the first step in liking your customers is to make it acceptable to like them.

Show the customers you like them

It should be much easier to like your customers if you talk about them in positive terms within your team and your organization. And if you genuinely like them, it should be fairly easy to show it. The important thing is that *everyone* shows it in *every* encounter with a customer. The techniques for doing this are very straightforward, especially if the liking is genuine:

- Smile when you greet customers, over the phone or face-to-face. Show you're pleased to talk to them.

- Give the impression that you want to help them.

- Find genuine opportunities to indicate that you like their tastes, choices or behavior: 'Yes, I like that sofa too' for example. Or 'Thank you for giving us plenty of notice; it makes a big difference to us.' Avoid empty flattery, but bother to express genuine feelings when they are positive towards the customer.

It is particularly important that, as a manager, you set an example of how to like your customers. Dumb managers think they can tell their team how to behave and then carry on as before themselves. But you need to set an example so that your team members feel they want to follow it in order to earn your approval.

It won't be long before you all start to realize that you really *do* like your customers a whole lot better than you used to. Your customers will sense this, and will respond in a friendly and co-operative way. Soon, you'll all want to give your customers the best service you can because, dammit, you like them and you want to help.

What if you really don't like your customers?
OK, fair enough. The occasional customer is just a bloody-minded sod. But very, very few customers will be genuinely difficult and unlikable in the face of good customer service. If they see that you like them and want to help, why should they need to be? Most 'difficult' customers are responding to a lack of co-operation on your part. If you appear not to

care about them, or are unwilling to be flexible to accommodate them, or are obstructive or uninterested in them, they are likely to be difficult in order to get through to you.

But even if they start annoyed or drunk or bad tempered, it doesn't take much to remain on good terms with them if you simply show an interest in them, look at the situation from their perspective, and show that you want to help. See past the difficult attitude they present you with, and focus on the underlying request or problem. If you are smart about understanding people, you will have noticed that some of your team seem to encounter far more difficult customers than others do. This says a great deal more about your individual team members than it does about your customers.

So long as you focus on the problem rather than on the customer's behavior, you can almost always find something to like if you try hard enough. Even if you can only make it as far as feeling sorry for a customer, at least you can find it in you to be kind and helpful towards them (without, of course, indicating that you feel pity towards them). See it as a challenge to find something likeable about them, and show enough interest in them for them to reveal their likeable side.

Show your customers they are important

Your customers must know that they matter to you. And it's not enough to assume that this is obvious to them; not when your competitors are pursuing them offering to make it more obvious than you do.

Get personal

One of the keys to showing customers they are important is recognizing that they are individuals. They don't want to know that they are one of hundreds or thousands. Each one wants his or her own individuality acknowledged. One of the simplest ways to do this is to address them by name. That doesn't simply mean addressing them by name over the phone or to their face, but sending out personalized letters and mailshots.

Bear in mind, too, that some customers – particularly younger ones – would prefer to be addressed by their Christian names. So encourage your team to use their own judgement. Don't have a company policy that all customers should be addressed as Mr or Mrs or Miss. Have a policy that all customers should be addressed in the way that the person dealing with them feels that they would like to be addressed.

When it comes to treating customers as individuals, your database is crucial. And it should be obvious why it matters that it is kept accurate. It would be better not to address a customer by name at all than to get their name wrong. Most customers will give you a chance to correct it, but if you get it wrong again you are telling them that it doesn't really matter to you whether you get their name right or not. Hardly very encouraging.

> *Smart things to say about customers*
>
> Customers may be inclined to blame an error on 'the computer' the first time. But if they point it out to you and the error is repeated, they will blame it on you.

The database also enables you to show you know your customers individually in other ways. You can mail them saying 'As one of our founder customers ...' or 'With your experience as a parent' or 'You'll recognize, as a senior manager ...'. You can let them know that you know them and take an interest in them.

Make them offers

As well as the respect you show by being personal with your customers, you should also acknowledge their importance in other ways. Make them offers which you make only to your regular customers. Make them feel special for being a customer; prospects aren't getting this offer, it's only for the really special people – your existing customers.

You might like to make the offer specific to certain groups of customer such as subscribers only, or customers who have been with you longer than five years, or customers who spend more than a certain amount with you each year. You can offer a free gift with their next order, or a discount. Let them know that far from being an incentive to become a customer, the offer won't be made to non-customers at all.

When it comes to discounts, these don't work so well for business customers. After all, it is their company, not themselves, who will benefit. Always remember that you are dealing with people. Make offers to business people which benefit them personally; free gifts should appeal to the individual, such as a luxury leather blotter or a travel case, perhaps.

Another way of letting customers feel important is to offer them the best option you have for something. Advance booking for something likely to be oversubscribed, for example. Or you might reserve your best seats – in a restaurant, airline, theatre or whatever – for existing customers.

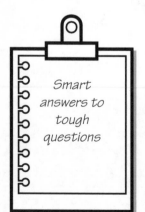

Smart answers to tough questions

Q: Why should we reward the individual rather than the business? Isn't that a bribe? The individual doesn't pay us a penny out of their own pocket for our products.

A: Whose influence and goodwill do you want to cultivate to win repeat business? Who is showing us the loyalty we are rewarding? And what is the business if not its people?

SMART
PEOPLE
TO HAVE ON
YOUR SIDE:

ARCHIE
NORMAN

SMART PEOPLE TO HAVE ON YOUR SIDE: ARCHIE NORMAN

- Politician and ex-chief executive of Asda.
- Believed it should be fun both to work and to shop at Asda.
- 'About 40 percent of the population never really smiles, and if they never smile then forget it. They shouldn't be in our business.'

Maybe you are holding a popular event and tickets are available only to customers.

The advantage of all these techniques is that they demonstrate to the customer how important they are *even if they don't take advantage of them*. You have made your point: you, as a customer, take top priority for us. We consider you to be extremely important and special, and we want you to know it.

The telephone is also an invaluable tool for showing customers they matter. Suppose a customer is staging a big event or exhibition, for which they have ordered one of your products. It may not be a business customer, it might be a private customer holding a big party or a wedding. Call them up afterwards to ask how it went. You don't have to be on intimate terms with a big account customer to do this. Anyone taking an order from any customer who discovers that this is the case can simply make a note in their diary to call the customer at the appropriate time.

And how about getting really personal? Seriously, some computer systems incorporate a facility for staff to write a personal message on any invoice which goes out. These tend to be used for messages like 'As discussed, the P57x is out of stock and will be forwarded after Jan 18th.' Very useful, but why not use it for other messages too, when it's appropriate? What about 'Good luck with the driving test' or 'Have a great holiday in the Seychelles'. If the person taking the order has elicited the fact that the customer has a driving test or a holiday coming up, let them know you were listening and you remembered.

Show an interest

The last point should have given smart managers a clue to another way of making customers feel important. Let them talk about themselves. This doesn't mean encouraging your team to chat for hours on the phone, but train them to listen for clues that enable them to talk to the customer as an individual. So if the customer says 'It's no good delivering it next week, I'll be on holiday', establish the best delivery time but also ask them where they are off to. If they tell you they will need a dog guard fitted in the car they are ordering from you, ask them what kind of dog they have.

People love to talk about themselves, as we all know, so let them do it. It doesn't have to take more than a moment, and the extra time it takes is more than worth it if it makes the customer feel liked and important.

Give your customers attention

As well as communicating with your customers when they get in touch, or when you make regular mailings or phone calls, an unsolicited contact can count for a huge amount. Everyone likes attention, so make sure your customers get that little bit of extra attention they deserve.

We all tend to phone our friends every so often just to say 'I haven't spoken to you for a while. How are you?' So why treat our customers

'I work in dispatch, and I really enjoy calling up customers to check a delivery went smoothly. If I didn't do it, I'd hardly speak to a customer from one week to the next.'

any differently? You don't have to have an excuse to contact them, but you might find it easier to start the call if you do. It doesn't matter which department you manage, and whether you have regular contact with your customers anyway. You and your team can call up customers anytime to check they are happy.

You can call up after delivering an order to say 'Did everything go OK? Were you happy with the service?' As we saw earlier, this is one way to unearth complaints, but it also reassures your happy customers that you care. You can make this sort of call from the sales office or the marketing department, but also from production, from despatch or from accounts.

One of the important things about this approach is that you are not trying to sell anything. The customer can see that this call is for their benefit, not yours. You can, however, also contact customers with a soft sell approach, either by phone or by letter, and still make them feel that you are paying them attention rather than trying to get money out of them. Do this by picking opportunities which are in their interests as well as yours, and which don't push them into responding with an order. For example:

- Let them know about a special offer specially aimed at customers like them (long-standing ones, or frequent orderers or whatever).

- Remind them that they usually place an order at this time of year, and perhaps remind them what they ordered last time (without ruling out the possibility of them increasing the order this time, of course).

- Write to a customer whose organization you know has recently restructured and check whether you need to update your contact details for them – are they still at the same office? Are they still using the same ordering system?

Don't push it; no one wants to be pestered constantly, but make sure you make unsolicited contact with your customers a couple of times a year to show them that you haven't forgotten them.

Recognize and appreciate your customers

All but the very dumbest managers around appreciate their customers, but for some reason only the smart ones actually bother to tell the customers so. As with any other kind of relationship, it helps to say 'Thanks for being there' from time to time. There are plenty of ways of doing this:

- send your customers a Christmas card

- hold events or exhibitions and send them free tickets

- invite them to the races or Wimbledon or some other entertainment as a thank you

- send them a gift.

When it comes to sending gifts, which most businesses do at Christmas, you need to make sure that the value of the gift reflects the value of their custom, or you will insult their loyalty. If they spend several thousand pounds a year with you, don't send them a biro with your company name printed on it, or a cheap calendar. And if they are business customers, send them something which will appeal to them person-ally. How about two bottles of really good vintage wine? Or tickets for Covent Garden?

Make sure your customers like you

In the last chapter we looked at how much more likely customers are to complain, rather than simply leave, if they like you. They will give you a second chance. But being likeable doesn't only help to unearth complaints, it makes your customers far more loyal. They don't want to leave if they like you; they'd miss you. And the replacement supplier they choose may be well priced, and give them plenty of attention and all the rest of it, but they might not actually like them. They might find them arrogant or overly formal or brusque – and these things count for a lot.

Smart quotes

'Be everywhere, do every-thing, and never fail to astonish the customer.'

Macy's motto

How to make people like you

In the last chapter we talked about having likeable people for your customers to deal with, and this is ab-solutely crucial. But there are other ways of backing this up as an organization. As a manager, you need to be aware of every opportunity you have to influence the way your customers see you, and to make sure that every time, you are positively influencing the customer to like you. Here are a few examples of opportunities to per-suade customers that they like you.

Smart things to say about customers

If your customers like you as an organization and as individuals it is extremely difficult for them to drag themselves away from you.

SMART PEOPLE TO HAVE ON YOUR SIDE: ALAN JONES

- Chief executive of TNT
- A very popular boss of a very popular company
- Believes that employees must be highly motivated in order to be able to give top class customer service
- Through his belief that service is everything, TNT has won numerous awards for quality.

- *Visiting your offices.* We all judge by appearances, but certain dumb managers seem to think that this rule excludes customers. It doesn't. Your offices should be smart, clean, tidy and friendly. This doesn't have to mean luxury if you can't afford it, but it's worth affording comfort for your customers. When they first arrive, if you have a car park, make sure the spaces nearest the entrance to the building are reserved for customers, not for the MD – and that for any member of the company to park in them is treated as a cardinal sin. Customers don't like having to walk further through the cold and wet just because senior management have got the best parking spaces. Let the MD get cold for a change. And signpost the parking and the entrance clearly.

The reception area should be comfortable and convenient. Don't stick your crappy old chairs out there; give them new ones selected for comfort as well as looks. Provide something for the customer to read – leave clean copies of catalogues or trade publications out, but give them a publication they like, too. Keep a copy of *Private Eye* or *The Week* in reception. They'll like you for giving them something enjoyable to read, rather than just the usual informative bumf.

Of course the reception staff should be friendly, helpful and efficient, and so should any other staff who happen to walk through the reception area when there is a customer there. If everyone who walks through gives them a friendly smile, it will make them feel special. Obviously customers should always be offered a cup of tea or coffee when they arrive. And go that little bit extra – give them a couple of decent chocolate biscuits with it.

Don't forget the loos. They should be pleasantly decorated and presentable, kept clean and well stocked – don't ever run out of toilet paper. And again, add the odd extra. A make up shelf and decent lighting for the women, and maybe some cotton wool balls. And add a likeable touch: entertaining cartoons on the wall, for example. If you make people laugh, they like you.

Smart quotes

'From this day forward, I solemnly promise and declare that every time a customer comes within ten feet of me I will smile, look him in the eye, and greet him, so help me Sam.'

Sam Walton

- *Receiving your catalogue.* A catalogue is a terrific opportunity to show how likeable you are. The copy you write gives you an opportunity to put your corporate personality across, so make it fun. Of course some products and customers require a different brand of fun from others, but be chatty. Make each customer feel you are talking to them one-to-one.

Your catalogue should be as easy as possible for your customers to find their way around. Include a contents list and, if the catalogue contains a lot of products, an index as well. Print item reference codes and prices where you think the customer wants them, not where it suits you. Print the price next to the product, not on a separate list. Yes, it can be more expensive, but your customers are worth it.

Once again, add those little extras the customer never even hoped for. Put items down in the index several times if the customer might want to look them up under any one of several names. Some catalogue companies print a ruler, in inches and centimeters, along the top of one of the pages so that when they quote the size of an item the customer can see exactly what 8" × 3.5" really looks like.

- *Correspondence from you.* As well as sending out mailshots, you often find yourself writing to customers individually in response to letters from them, or to set up appointments, or to answer queries or complaints. Needless to say, all letters should be written and sent out quickly; don't keep the customer waiting. In fact, aim to surprise them by replying to them faster than they had hoped.

Make sure these letters are as chatty and individual as possible. (Don't say 'Reference your letter of the 13th inst.') Write in simple, straightforward language, and look for opportunities to treat the customer as an individual. For example: 'I thoroughly enjoyed our meeting yesterday; I do hope you managed to catch that train in the end.'

- *Routine paperwork.* How many times have you found yourself ploughing through bits of paper you didn't want from suppliers? Why do they send you the green bit as well as the pink one? And where on the invoice are you supposed to find the actual amount owed? Your customers don't want your paperwork. They may need it, but they still don't want it. So keep it as simple as possible, and send them only what they might need to have, before they start wanting to tell you where to stick your duplicates.

Keep your paperwork simple and readable. Only include the information which is necessary, and make it really easy to find. And even official paperwork can be friendly. Just because this is an invoice, it doesn't mean to say you can't address the customer as 'you'. Don't say 'If unsatisfied, this product should be returned, in its original packaging, using the returns form overleaf ...'. Be friendly and likeable. How about 'If you're not entirely happy with this product, please send it back to us and we'll replace or refund it for you. You'll find a returns form and pre-paid postage label over the page. We'd be grateful if you'd reuse the original packaging to return it in.'

> *Smart things to say about customers*
>
> Keep your style friendly and informal. If you wouldn't say it to the customer's face, don't write it.

- *Deliveries.* Your customers expect you to send products promptly, and well packaged so that they arrive undamaged. But if you think about how you feel about receiving and opening parcels you'll realize that there is more to it than that. Some are done up so that Houdini couldn't get into them, and can put you in a serious strop before you finally break into them. Sometimes the product is in good condition but the paperwork has disappeared or been crumpled up.

Some packages are valuable and need to be signed for. And if you're sending them to a business address, there should be someone there to take delivery. But if you're sending deliveries to home addresses it can be very difficult for the customer if they are out and work all day but you've decided to use a delivery service which means they have to sign for the package. So find an alternative, or give them a choice on the order form – let them fill in what they would like the delivery service to do if they are out when the parcel is delivered.

And don't forget all those likeable extras you can add to make life more pleasant for your customers when they receive deliveries from you. *Lakeland* put a 'thank you for ordering from us' card in with every parcel they send out. Some organizations specially wrap their parcels the old-fashioned way with brown paper and string to make it more exciting to open (this obviously works better for sending out gifts than for sending a fresh supply of ½" screws to a manufacturer).

So these are just a few examples of how to take positive steps to make sure your customers find you convenient to do business with and actively like you. As you can see, they spread across all departments of the organization; this, of course, is essential since you cannot afford to send your customers mixed messages. They must like your entire organization, so everyone has to find ways in which their own section or department can be as likeable as possible.

Building customer loyalty is essential to make it as difficult as possible for your competitors to steal your customers away from you. The smart approach is to recognize that your customers are people, and have human wants and needs:

• show them you like them

• treat them with respect and importance

- give them attention

- recognize and appreciate their custom

- make them like you.

Understanding customers as people is the skill which dumb managers seem to lack. Grasp it yourself, and you're firmly in the smart set. And achieving an ever lower customer turnover will confirm that you know your stuff.

6

Relationship Marketing

It's the latest buzz phrase in marketing – 'relationship marketing'. And like most trendy buzz phrases, it gives away precious little about what it actually means. Is it just a passing fad, or is it really here to stay? And what is it anyway?

Well, to start with, it's here to stay. And despite the hype and the fad image, it is a genuinely effective approach to customer service which takes account management into a completely new sphere, where you can have a personal relationship with every one of your customers. It is, at least for now, the ultimate tool for building customer loyalty.

Smart quotes

'Customer-driven competition is what we call one-to-one marketing, a form of marketing that was prohibitively expensive, and therefore nearly inconceivable, to the traditional marketer just a few years ago.'

Peppers and Rogers

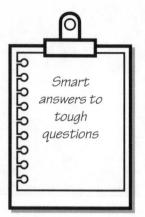

Smart
answers to
tough
questions

Q: Aren't loyalty-building techniques already pretty sophisticated? Do we need to create a completely new approach to something which already works very well?

A: Customers expect what they are taught to expect. And the future will teach us all to expect far more as customers than we could hope for now. This huge rise in expectations will demand a radical change in everyone's approach to customer loyalty.

What is it?

Relationship marketing – sometimes referred to as 'customer relationship management – has developed out of advances in information technology. It has always been possible to have an intimate relationship with your customers if you have only a few big clients. But it has not been possible to be close to each and every customer if your customer base runs into thousands and tens of thousands. Now it is.

But relationship marketing is not simply about investing in new technology. It's not just a case of buy the latest, snazziest database and hey, presto! you're a relationship marketeer. Relationship marketing is about adopting a completely new mindset about your customers and how you interact with them; it also involves restructuring the organization to maximize the possibilities of customer service.

Up until now, organizations have been essentially focused on their products. Even the most customer-oriented companies have taken the product as the starting point and then looked around for customers to sell it to. Those companies which are smart about customer service have made the product as likeable and as well packaged with extras as they can, but the product is still the starting point. The organization is still engaged in mass marketing to its customers.

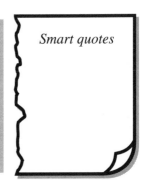
'The customer only wants to know what the product or service will do for him tomorrow. All he is interested in are his own values, his own wants, his own reality. For this reason alone, any serious attempt to state what our business is must start with the customer, his realities, his situation, his behavior, his expectations, and his values.'

Peter Drucker

Relationship marketing turns this approach on its head. You have to start with the customer – each customer individually – and find out what they want. Then supply it. No more marketing to your customers *en masse*; it's time for a one-to-one relationship with each customer. No longer are you concerned with measuring your share of the total market, the aim is to increase your share of each customer's total spend.

One of the buzz phrases to grow out of relationship marketing is 'mass customization'; in other words, finding ways to customize your products and services for each one of your customers. Again, this can be achieved only if you begin by focusing on the customer and their needs, rather than on your own products or services.

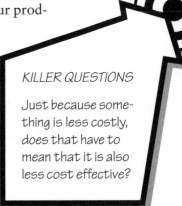

KILLER QUESTIONS

Just because something is less costly, does that have to mean that it is also less cost effective?

Your image of your customer

To embrace relationship marketing, you must look at customers in a completely different light. The traditional approach to marketing is segmentation: divide customers into groups or segments which have a lot in common, and then find products you can sell to the whole group. This is less costly, it is argued, than treating customers individually.

The relationship-marketing approach is to look at each customer individually. Relationship marketeers certainly look at market segments to find out what customers have in common, but they don't do so in order to serve those customers as a group. They do so in order to gain an insight into each individual customer's needs and tastes. By doing this, it is possible to anticipate what a customer will want before they know it themselves, because you have observed that other, similar customers want it.

As analysis software has become more sophisticated, organizations have begun to break their traditional marketing approach down into smaller and smaller segments. Rather than dividing customers into business and consumer, as they might have done 10 or 20 years ago, they now subdivide them into more and more units. In one sense, you might think they were moving closer and closer to relationship marketing.

But the smart thinker will see that they are not. Even if you could create segments with a single customer in each, you would still have missed the point of relationship marketing. And the point is that market segments and individual people are two completely different things, and we treat them in completely different ways.

- If you adopt segmentation marketing, the main thrust of your approach is to analyze behavior and then project future behavior as a result. Segments are essentially passive, static, predictable things.

- With relationship marketing, the approach is to seek feedback and then

Smart things
to say about
customers

Segmentation is about defining the *average* customer in each segment and then catering to them. But the 'average' customer doesn't actually exist. Relationship marketing is concerned only with customers who really exist.

customize individually. One-to-one relationships are dynamic, fluid and interactive.

This should affect how you see your customers. The traditional view is to see each customer as one of a category, for example aged 60+, retired, with a good level of disposable income and an interest in gardening and cooking. But this kind of classification, although it has great value at times as we have seen, is only useful for the light it sheds on individual customers. The prime view of each customer should be as a single living, breathing person. What do they look like? What are their politics? What is their favorite food? What kind of holidays do they enjoy? Do they like cats?

You may never learn all this information about each of your customers. If you have thousands or millions of customers you certainly won't. That doesn't matter. What matters is that you undergo a sea change in the way you view and describe your customers. Stop seeing them as an example of a category or segment, and start seeing them as real people.

Building loyalty

This is the way to reinforce customer loyalty, and cementing customer loyalty is the key to profitability; it means lower marketing costs and a more efficient operation. Interestingly, research shows that customer satisfaction and customer loyalty are not the same thing, although dissatisfied customers are – not surprisingly – unlikely to show much loyalty. But customers perceive two different types of quality: functional quality and technical quality. Functional quality covers customer service factors such as responsiveness and empathy, while technical quality is all about the performance and reliability of the product.

> **Smart things to say about customers**
>
> We tend to talk about quality as though it were an objectively measurable thing. But the definition of quality varies from one customer to the next.

Most customers will give you a satisfaction rating based on one of these types of quality (you won't know which one unless you ask). But their loyalty will be dependent on the other factor. So for the customer, the two factors taken together create the whole picture. This means that you cannot create customer loyalty simply by creating customer satisfaction, although satisfaction is a prerequisite for loyalty. So your customer satisfaction measures, although essential, aren't giving you the whole picture. What is also clear, however, is that relationship marketing completes the equation for you, generating loyalty to run alongside the satisfaction.

That old database thing again

Relationship marketing has only become possible since the development of cleverer and more advanced databases using CRM (customer relationship management) software. The database enables you to do three vital things:

- It enables you to know each one of your customers and to hold information about each individually. The database can give you a detailed record of complex interactions with each one of hundreds of thousands of customers. And it can do it in a moment.

- It also enables customers to communicate with you, and to tell you what they want – it is interactive. Transaction data tells the database what products, add-ons and so on this customer likes. The database knows how often the customer likes to order, and when. But the customer can add to this information. They can call up the database and give it more information; this is how home grocery shopping works. The customer gives the store database its regular shopping list, and then simply adapts the basic list for each separate order. If your customers' own technology is not as advanced as yours, you can mail questionnaires to your customers and invite them to give you the information they want your database to have.

- You can customize products and services as a routine part of your operation using mass customization technology. Your computer can tell your despatch department about the specialized addressing requirements of a particular customer, or pass on to the production department details of the customized features this particular customer always wants on this particular product.

It should be becoming clear why modern technology has been driving the revolution in relationship marketing. Only now, as these technologies develop, is it possible to have a one-to-one relationship with each of your customers.

Smart answers to tough questions

> Q: Just because a customer *can* interact with us, it doesn't mean they want to. Why should they want to give us personal information about themselves?
>
> A: Because it is our job to see that when they do, it has direct, recognizable benefits for them. We need to give them results in order to provide an incentive for them to keep giving us the data.

The two-way relationship

So what's the difference to the customer? The essence of the whole approach is that your communications with your customer are two-way. That's what makes it a relationship. They don't have to wait for you to contact them; they can let you know what it is that they want when it suits them. As well as the information you glean from interactions with them and from their past history with you, they can take the initiative in adding to your store of knowledge about them. From their point of view, this saves them from having to repeat the information to you each time they make an enquiry or place an order, and it enables them to give you additional information about extras, add-ons and customizations which they want.

This is the direction of the technology of the future in all sorts of spheres. It is only a matter of time before cars, for example, can give their drivers personal, interactive service – the first cars to do so are already coming off the production lines. To take cars as an example, in the next ten or twenty years you will be able to get into your car and it will recognize you by your weight, and distinguish you from any other member of your family who also drives it. As a result, it will adjust the seat and the controls and the mirrors to your favorite position. It will know what temperature you like the car to be, so it will adjust the heating or air-conditioning accordingly. It will set the radio to your favorite station. The car will know how you like to drive, and how you adapt to different outside driving conditions, so it will adjust the engine to perform as economically as possible for your personal driving style. And it will do all this because you have given it the information. If you change your taste in radio stations, or decide to adopt a different driving position, you will tell the car and it will adapt to suit you.

This is a truly interactive relationship between you and the car. What is more, the data from the car will be passed back to your dealer so that

> In the future, people will expect more and more products to be interactive. And one of the benefits of this interactivity will be that they will be in control of the data they do and don't choose to give. Control of the product will increasingly devolve to the customer.

Smart things to say about customers

when you change cars the replacement will be instantly programmed with all this information.

Imagine your customers being able to give you this kind of information about themselves, and your organization having the capability to record and process it. What is happening is that you are having a genuinely two-way, interactive relationship with your customer. At first glance, the idea of relationship marketing seems crazy, especially if you have hundreds of thousands of customers. However, what is really happening on a day-to-day basis is that your computer is having hundreds of thousands of one-to-one relationships.

This isn't a terribly fashionable way of putting it, by the way. Relationship marketing is supposed to be truly personal, and a computer isn't truly personal. But you are in control of the technology and the system, and you can pick up on any of your computer's intimate conversations at any time, so what's the problem?

The computer system is your basis for relationship marketing, but it can't be stressed enough that it is simply a tool; it may be the biggest and best

> If the computer system can give the customer exactly what they want, and in effect hold an intelligent conversation with them, *and* they can phone up and speak to one of us personally any time they like ... why would they care that they are sometimes talking to a machine and not a person?

KILLER QUESTIONS

tool you've ever had, but it can't do the job without you. You still need to contact your customers by phone, fax, mail and e-mail, to send them Christmas cards and phone up to check that their last order arrived OK and was satisfactory. Customer relationship management does not replace your previous relationship with your customers, it builds on it.

The key to loyalty

So why exactly is relationship marketing such a clever and effective way to build customer loyalty? You have to understand what it is that customers are loyal to. They don't buy from you out of any moral sense of duty or obligation. They don't stick with you because they feel they owe it to you. They don't even stay because your prices are low, as we saw in the last chapter. Loyalty and price are not related.

Smart quotes

'If we provide real satisfaction to real customers – we will be profitable.'

John Young

No. Frankly, your customers stay with you because it suits them to. Their loyalty is built on convenience and enjoyment. As we saw in the last chapter, there are plenty of aspects of functional quality which boost loyalty, such as liking the customer and giving them attention. And then there is technical quality; the performance and reliability of the product or service. To retain your competitive edge, you must widen the gap between you and your competitors – in your customers' eyes – as far as possible.

Relationship marketing sets up an interaction between you and your customer in which you are constantly learning from them. They teach you, step by step, exactly what they want – and you deliver it. This makes it far more convenient for them to stay with you than to desert you for another supplier: they would have to repeat the entire teaching process. And the longer they stay with you, the more you learn – and the more they would have to repeat if they left you.

There's another reason, too, why relationship marketing improves customer loyalty. It's the psychological angle. If your customer has invested time and effort into collaborating with you to teach you how to serve them best, they will inevitably feel that they have a stake in the relationship. They will have a bond with you which they were an equal partner in forging, and which they are therefore reluctant to walk away from.

In an effective relationship with a customer, the pair of you should be collaborating as partners to bring yourselves mutual benefits. You need to create a culture in which you are both on the same side. The customer is supplying the knowledge of what is needed and how, and you are supplying the product or service to fit the specification. Isn't that how you work with managers from other departments and sections? You each bring your own specialist knowledge, and between you, you find the best way forward. Relationship marketing is about setting up a collaborative partnership with each of your customers.

Customize, customize, customize

It should be clear from this that the more you can customize the service you give your customers, the more intimate your relationship with them

SMART PEOPLE
TO HAVE ON
YOUR SIDE:

DALE
CARNEGIE

SMART PEOPLE TO HAVE ON YOUR SIDE: DALE CARNEGIE

- Author of *How to Win Friends and Influence People*.
- A great communicator and a born salesman.
- Understood the principles of face-to-face communication like few others.
- Taught people how to like and be liked.

can become. And the closer the relationship, the greater the potential for loyalty.

In most organizations which haven't yet discovered relationship marketing, the most they may know about their customer is that they have a different delivery address from their billing address. Well, it's a start, but it's hardly enough to deter the customer from finding another supplier. Not a huge hassle for them to repeat this essential piece of personal data, really.

You need as much relevant data about your customer as possible – that is, data which *they* consider relevant – in order to give you a clear lead over your competitors. And, critically, you need information which surprises the customer. They must know that you can second-guess their needs in ways they hadn't anticipated – you can use the data you hold to give them benefits they couldn't ask another supplier for because they hadn't thought of it themselves.

For example, you might write to a business customer to say that you have developed a special offer. During your ongoing research into developments in their industry you know that there is a recent product which is ideal for companies of a particular size and type, which you know they fit. This latest technology is only available to customers with a particular type of compatible equipment. The customer, as you know, doesn't have this equipment, but you have developed a way of upgrading their existing equipment to make it compatible. You are therefore writing to offer them this upgrade at a special price.

You couldn't have written this letter without knowing a good deal about the customer, their industry and the equipment they run, and then putting all these pieces of data together to arrive at an offer which they didn't know was possible. It is this kind of creative use of the relationship marketing potential which makes it such an effective way of building business.

Customize creatively

There is another level of customization, though, which really clinches relationship marketing. Suppose you have a product which is more technologically advanced than your competitors. Perhaps you have developed a cooker which has all sorts of fancy programming capabilities. Maybe you can program it to switch the oven fan off an hour into the cooking time, or detect when something is burning and reduce the temperature.

When you first introduce these features – designed in response to researching what your customers most want – you have a product customized to suit your own customers' requests which gives you a competitive advantage. But it is only a matter of time before your competitors develop the same advances – and maybe more besides. And when they do, what is there to stop your customers switching to them? The traditional view is that you cannot stop your competitors duplicating your own ability to customize – perhaps even exceeding it – and then taking your customers from you.

Ha! The traditionalists are wrong. If you follow the relationship marketing approach, you *can* stop them. You need to think in terms of customizing to the individual, not to market segments. Suppose you develop a cooker which contains voice-recognition software. Each individual customer can program the cooker to cook any dish in any way. For example, they can program it to know that when they cook rice pudding they want it cooked for two hours in a slow oven, with the fan on for the last half-hour to help brown the top. All they have to do is to say 'rice pudding' as they put the

> 'Tomorrow's global and European markets will not be fragmented into the secure, predictable domestic bases we have known, but characterized by new and volatile trade patterns. In this environment it will be the creative ability to define new ways of looking at markets, products and consumers, and of managing people, which will be the hallmark of outstanding companies. No one will be spared the need to reappraise their activities.'
>
> *John Banham*

dish in the oven, and the cooker will do the rest. The next customer might cook their rice pudding in an hour in a hotter oven. Or even in a pan on top of the stove. Each customer can program in, say, up to a hundred cooking instructions which the cooker will recognize simply by hearing the name of the dish spoken by one of the recognized users.

Now, even if your competitors develop exactly the same technology, the customer is at a disadvantage if they go and buy it. If they upgrade their cooker to a new model of yours, they can remove the microchip from the old cooker, install it in the new one, and all the information is still there. But if they buy one of your competitors' cookers, even with the same technology, they will have to program in all that information all over again. You have given yourself a permanent competitive advantage. And an advantage which grows every time the customer programs in the instructions for a new recipe. You have made yourself all but indispensable.

What if you can't customize?

Many dumb managers sit around at this point and say 'Aha, just as I thought. Relationship marketing isn't really for us. We don't have the sort of product you can customize. All we sell is metal screws in six different sizes and three different materials, and most of our customers regularly buy several of our products. Nope, not much scope there for customizing. Relationship marketing sounds great for other companies, but it wouldn't work for us.'

Wrong. The arguments for customizing speak for themselves: the more you can customize the greater your customers' loyalty will be. It's a fact. So if the route to customizing isn't obvious, the answer is not to abandon it but to ask 'How can we get in on this?'

And there's an answer. You don't have to customize the product itself. You can customize the service that goes with it. You can customize the packaging, the despatch method, the payment system. You can customize the way you deal with the customer – whether you contact them to remind them that their regular order is due, and how often you do so; how often you visit them; what time of day you phone them. Relationship marketing calls for

creativity; as we saw before, the data is only as good as the use you put it to. Smart managers will recognize that customizing is perfectly possible whatever your line of business, and whatever your own department, but it's your job to create opportunities to do it.

The value of your customer

If you're smart, you'll be thinking by now 'This all sounds lovely. But

where on earth is the money going to come from for all these changes?'
Well, in the long term, relationship marketing is a necessary and valuable
route for most businesses – certainly those with large customer bases, unless you happen to be a monopoly with no threat of competition. So implementing relationship marketing is not a matter of 'if' but 'how'. For the
next few years you may get away with putting it off, at least if your competitors are also slacking, but in the end it will become the standard marketing approach. And how much better to make the move ahead of your
competitors and be ahead of the race when it begins in earnest. Relationship marketing will become standard because:

- it is there, and once one organization does it, its competitors will have
  to do it to keep up

- the technology is there, and improving all the time

- it works, by giving both a competitive edge which
  builds customer satisfaction by delivering exactly what
  the customer wants, and customer loyalty by making the
  customer increasingly reliant on your knowledge of them.

But the question still remains: how do you spend resources
you haven't got? And the answer is: you prioritize. You cannot
hope to offer every conceivable customization at once; you need
to offer the most valuable ones at first and, as this generates
resources, use them to determine the next options to incorporate. So you need to decide how to prioritize.

And the answer lies with your customers. Once you see your customers as individuals, not as groups, you can value each of them
individually. This is crucial because you can then see your customers in terms of their value relative to each other. Whilst you

would like, in an ideal world, to offer everything possible to all your customers, in the real world this isn't possible. So first, offer those customized features which your most valuable customers want. Ask them: survey them by mail and by phone, establish what more you can do for them. Supplying their needs – through the whole gamut of marketing techniques, not only relationship marketing – may well supply those of your less valuable customers too. But even if it doesn't, at least you have satisfied the customers you most need to satisfy and build loyalty in.

Value your customers. That sounds like a nice easy statement. But there are almost as many ways of valuing a customer as there are customers. So which is the most effective? In fact, there are two key values you need to establish for each of your customers: their current value and their potential value.

Current value

The most effective way to value a customer is to calculate their lifetime value; the amount they will be worth to you over the entire course of your relationship with them. In other words, the revenue you would lose if you lost the customer. This valuation takes into account:

- the profits on all future transactions with the customer ...

- minus the costs of those transactions and the wider costs of servicing the customer (phone calls, mailshots and so on)

- plus the value of any referrals to new customers

- plus the value of any help in designing products, improving customer service, or contributing to any other profitable developments.

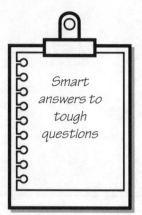

Q: Surely it's possible for a customer to have a negative value: to be costing more than they are worth to the organization. What do you do then?

A: Be grateful you found out – thanks to a relationship-driven approach. Establish whether you can increase their value and, if you can't, get rid of them.

Of course you cannot know exactly what all these factors amount to, but software for making this kind of calculation is becoming increasingly sophisticated. Many factors will need to be assumed as an average – such as the total duration of the relationship with the customer – but the software will be able to calculate an average for a particular type of customer rather than calculating only the average across the entire customer base and feeding this in to every individual customer calculation.

Potential value

The potential value of each of your customers is always as high or higher than their current value. It represents their current value *plus* any value you are not getting but might potentially win from them. Imagine you manufacture tinned peas and beans – baked beans, haricot beans, tins of peas and so on. You sell them to supermarket chains. One of your customers, a big chain of stores, buys all their baked beans from you. You can calculate their current value to you on the basis of those baked beans sales.

But what if you could persuade them to buy their other peas and beans from you as well, instead of from your competitors? You can't calculate these sales into your current valuation because you aren't currently making the sales. But what about the potential for the growth of business with this supermarket chain? The potential valuation for each customer takes this into account as well.

At the beginning of this chapter, we saw that the way to view relationship marketing is to focus not on increasing your market share, but on increasing your share of each individual customer. Calculating the potential value of each customer is what enables you to do this.

Using your customer valuations

You need to establish both values for each of your customers because the difference between the two will determine your strategy towards that customer. If their current value is high, and their potential value little higher, you have a very valuable customer, but one in whom there is not much more growth potential. So your strategy should be to focus on retaining the customer. All your marketing efforts should be directed towards increasing their loyalty towards you.

But suppose the current value of a customer is a lot lower than their potential. Perhaps it is a lot lower than most of your customers, but their potential is high. Perhaps, while being one of your least profitable customers at the moment, they have the potential to be one of the most profitable. Maybe you are in car sales. They buy their directors' cars from you, but not the cars for their entire sales staff of a hundred people. You want them to buy these cars from you as well; that is their unrealized potential as a customer. In this case, your strategy should be to focus on growth rather than simply retention. This is a customer you want to entice away from your competitors until you have maximized their potential with you.

So focus on both these groups of customers when you prioritize your marketing resources into customizing products and services for your customers. If you concentrate only on retaining those customers with the highest current valuation, you are excluding the option of expanding business with those customers whose potential may be even higher.

> **Smart things to say about customers**
>
> Unless we know our customers' current and potential values, we don't know whether to focus our strategy on retention or growth.

Restructuring for relationships

Any smart manager should have worked out by now that such a dramatic change of approach to customers must call for dramatic changes in the whole structure of the organization. For a start you and your fellow managers must all share a vision of where you are going. You must all agree that relationship marketing is the way forward, and you must be ready to train and inspire your teams. Most important of all, the MD or CEO must be fully behind the shift in culture. Most drives towards relationship marketing which fail do so because the very top management lack the vision or the enthusiasm to see it through.

Smart quotes

> 'If your evaluation of consumer need is wrong you will of course end up making the product for the wrong market and will be selling it in the wrong way. You can invest in as much plant as you like, your production efficiency can be awe-inspiring, but you will be wasting your time.'
>
> *Sir David Orr*

Very often, making a switch to relationship marketing calls for a significant investment in information technology. You must be able to collect, store and access all the information you are going to need on each customer in order to customize your service to them. And you will need the capability to integrate new technology products as they emerge. For example, the time will probably come when you want your customers to be able to add information to your database via their PC, or to program a voice fingerprint on to your records – so you can supply any new voice-recognition products already programmed to respond to their own voice.

But perhaps the biggest change of all will be in the structure of the organization. Most large organizations, and many small ones, are structured for their own benefit. They are organized by product or by function. Perhaps the sales and maintenance sections are completely separate. Often a customer will be treated as two different entities if they buy products from two different sections of the company. Suppose they work from home and have two phone lines – one business and one domestic. They may be treated as two separate customers by the 'business' and 'domestic' sections of the phone company. And if they buy a phone from 'business sales' they may not be recognized when they contact 'business maintenance' to report a fault.

In one-to-one, or relationship, marketing you must organize the company according to customers. The old divisions must be integrated so that the individual relationship with each customer can be followed through regardless of the reason for the contact with them.

So how do you structure the organization? Don Peppers and Martha Rogers, authors of *The One-to-One Future* and highly successful relationship-marketing consultants, propose a model in which you tier your customers according to their value, and then group them into portfolios of customers with similar needs. These are not market segments, but groups of individual customers. Each of these groups is the responsibility of a customer manager, whose job is to manage the complete relationship with each customer and to increase the value of each to the organization. The customer manager oversees all communications and dialogue with each customer, and finds new products or services to sell to each of them, and new ways to customize to each one's specifications. The customer deals only with the customer manager and their team, regardless of whether they want to make a complaint, report a maintenance problem, make a purchase or hold a dialogue to increase the company's value to them.

The customer managers need people to tell them what can be done, and to work out how to do it. These people are the capabilities managers. The

capability manager's job is to make sure that the organization *can* deliver what the customer manager determines that it *should* deliver. They are responsible for overseeing production, logistics, delivery and service.

Is it working?

Many traditional ways of measuring success don't apply in relationship marketing. It's no good, for example, simply measuring the number of transactions. In the long term, of course, the aim is to increase the value of the existing customer base. But how do you measure this in the short term?

You need to use customer-based measures, such as current and potential valuations of each customer. There are other measures, too, which you can use. For example:

- Customer retention, although this interrelates with new customer acquisition, so you must view all the relevant figures. Which customers are you losing: the new ones, or the long term ones, or a particular type of customer?

- And you will still need to measure customer satisfaction, although with the understanding that this isn't the same thing as customer loyalty.

- Another important measure is your share of the customer's total spend. Suppose you sold one customer £50,000-worth of cars last year. You might be very pleased with yourself. But perhaps that organization actually spent £500,000 on cars last year. So you only captured a ten percent share of the customer's budget.

The key thing is to find ways to measure the profitability of each customer, and to focus on the profitability of customers, not products.

Making the change

It is clear that the restructuring involved in making the culture change to relationship marketing can be huge and disruptive. But it isn't necessary to do it all at once.

The way to make a gradual transition to relationship marketing is to start by introducing the new approach for just a few customers; those which are most valuable to you. Your organization may already be managing these as key accounts. Senior management should then appoint the smartest, most creative people as customer managers.

> **Smart things to say about customers**
>
> Massive disruption tends to demoralize people and if the results aren't very obvious, very fast, the whole drive for change can lose pace and enthusiasm.

As the benefits start to emerge and, as the system settles down, add a few more of your next most valuable customers to the system. Again, the customer manager's job is to:

- make sure that all data on each customer is linked up, even if they are dealing with different sections of the organization, or different regional branches.

- calculate the current and potential value of each customer, and the organization's share of customer, and establish other ways to measure success for each customer such as volume of orders, satisfaction, spread to buying new lines or whatever seems appropriate.

- find out how each customer prefers to communicate, see that these are the methods used, and oversee the effectiveness of these communications.

- interact with each customer to establish ways of customizing which will make it more convenient for the customer to do business with the organization.

- find ways to make the effort of collaboration worth the customer's while by using the information they give to cross-sell other products or services to them.

As each phase of new customers is successfully integrated into relationship marketing, and the positive results start to show, phase in the next level of customers. In this way, the transition to relationship marketing will create minimum disruption in the organization, and for maximum gain.

7

Win New Customers

Almost throughout this book, we've seen how it is important to put resources into retaining customers, not into recruiting new
ones. Now, suddenly, here's a whole chapter about winning new customers. What's going on?

Well, it's a matter of priorities. The most important, and
most cost-effective, way to run a business is to concentrate on keeping the customers you've got rather than
creating new ones. And, as we saw in the last chapter
especially, you can increase your business by increasing the value of your existing customers. But winning
new customers is still important:

Smart quotes

'You can automate the
production of cars, but you
cannot automate the production of customers.'

Walter Reuther

- If you are a young, growing business, you will never have any customers if you don't start by winning them.

- If you are in an industry where your customers hit a recession – whether or not you do – you will inevitably have a high customer fallout rate, which needs to be compensated for.

- In any business, no matter how successful, you are bound to suffer some customer fallout.

- There is a limit to how far you can increase business if you restrict yourself to your existing customers, even though that limit may be very far off at the moment.

> *Smart things to say about customers*
>
> The only way to have a potential for unlimited growth is to have an unlimited market.

So winning new customers is important, after all. Given the choice, it is better to double the business from one customer than to go out and get another customer. It costs less, and it generally implies a more satisfied customer who is getting more of what they want from you. But if you can multiply your business with them *and* have another equally valuable customer too ... hey, go for it. Just make sure you get the priorities in the right order.

There's another reason for this order of importance. If you don't focus on satisfying your existing customers as your top priority, you'll find that you lose more of them. And you lose more of the *new* customers you just invested in going out and winning. That's a terrific method of throwing your money away. So get your house in order first. Consolidate the customers you have, make sure they are as satisfied and as profitable as possible, and then worry about finding new ones. That way, the new customers will come into a culture which is already providing what its customers want, and is set up to increase loyalty very fast, and a far higher proportion of them will stay with you as long term, loyal and profitable customers. It's in your own interests as a manager to get this focus right, because it will make your department and your organization far more profitable.

So how do you win new customers? Regardless of what your business is, there are set stages you need to go through. Dumb managers think it's easy – you go out there and sell, don't you? Maybe a bit of advertising too? But the smarter manager understands that you need to plan your moves before you make them in order to ensure that you are being as economical as possible with all your resources. In particular, you should never lose sight of the enormous expense of recruiting new customers. You must do everything possible to manage the budget as wisely as possible.

There are six key steps to recruitment:

1. set your objectives

2. profile your existing customers

3. target your prospects

4. plan your approach

5. initiate contact

6. create the customer.

You must go through all these stages if you want to win new customers cost-effectively, and hold on to them once you have won them.

KILLER QUESTIONS

If we win new customers in order to turn them into loyal, long term customers, aren't we just focusing on our existing customer base anyway?

Smart things to say about customers

Winning new customers isn't about selling; it's about planning.

Set your objectives

As with any project or operation, the smart move is always to set a clear objective before you begin. The clearer you are at the outset about exactly where you're going, the more likely you are to get there, and to get there by the most direct and effective route. So begin by establishing precisely what you're trying to achieve. You want to end up with more customers than you have now, obviously. But that's not good enough. You need to come up with clear figures to aim for.

There are three figures you need to set before any customer recruitment campaign:

- the number of new customers you are planning to win

- the maximum acceptable cost of recruiting each new customer

- the overall budget.

These three figures are clearly interrelated. The dumb manager might imagine that you just want to win as many new customers as possible, but no doubt you will see that while that might be the case in an ideal world, it isn't a valid approach. You cannot budget if you don't know what you're aiming for, and you cannot know at the end of the campaign whether you've succeeded or not if you don't actually know what you were trying to do.

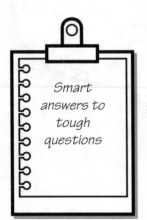

Smart answers to tough questions

Q: If we set out to win new customers, and we achieve that, surely we've succeeded haven't we?

A: Not if we could have achieved the same number of new customers at a lower cost, nor if each new customer costs so much to win that they may not pay for themselves fast enough to be worthwhile.

Face it: it costs a lot of money to win new customers. For all those you win, you carry the cost of those you targeted but failed to win. If you target, say, a thousand prospects and fifty of them become customers, each of those has effectively had to be worth the cost of another nineteen who didn't come through. Those fifty between them have to justify the cost of all the planning, time, communication, print and production costs, and overheads, for all thousand prospects you approached.

So before you begin you need to know how many customers you want to win, and indeed how many you need to win, to justify the overall costs. If you have your overall budget figure, that enables you to calculate how much you can afford to spend per prospect. And you need to know how many customers you expect to win as a result of the campaign so that you can estimate the cost per actual customer that you are allowing.

This applies whether you are launching a major customer recruitment drive or whether you have an ongoing campaign of seeking new customers. If the latter applies, you will simply need to calculate these figures for each budget period.

What if you don't get round to doing these calculations, or haven't the time, or hate figurework, or just can't be bothered?

> *Smart things to say about customers*
>
> Finding ways to spend money on customer recruitment isn't a problem. It costs as much as you are prepared to spend. So the vital thing to decide is: how much *are we prepared* to spend?

Without these figures, there is a danger that you will launch into an advertising, telephone or direct mail customer recruitment campaign which costs more than it could hope to win back in the value of the new customers it wins. You need to bear in mind that you will have to invest the money in the campaign well before you see any return on it. That doesn't just mean that you won't see any return until the end of the campaign. Often you won't pay back the investment until much later. Depending on your business, the initial sales income from the new customers whom you do succeed in winning will not necessarily pay back the cost of recruiting them. Each new customer may take several sales, over months or even years, to pay back your investment in them.

This is yet another reason why it is not worth investing too heavily in new customers until you have built up a level of customer service and customer satisfaction which ensures that, once you have captured a customer, they are likely to stay with you for a very long time. Contrary to what dumb managers believe, it is perfectly possible for a new customer to be worth less than no customer at all. After all, once you've won them, it will *still* cost you money to hang on to them.

KILLER QUESTIONS

If a customer is going to leave us before they have paid back our investment in them, why did we go out and recruit them in the first place?

Aim for the softest targets

Some new customers cost less to recruit than others. It all depends on how likely they are to start buying from you and how cheaply you can reach them. If you target very promising prospects, you might recruit one in ten of them – perhaps even more. If you target cold prospects, your hit rate might be as low as one in a hundred or even lower. This clearly makes a huge difference to the cost per new customer. The warm prospects only have to justify the cost of nine misses for each successful hit, while each of the cold prospects you win has to make the other 99 you failed to win worthwhile.

So who are the most likely prospects to convert to customers? If we divide prospects into seven categories, we can arrange them in order with those most likely to be successfully converted to customers at the top of the list, and the least promising at the bottom:

1. your own list of promising targets

2. customers' recommendations

3. ex-customers

4. prospects who have made enquiries but not yet bought

5. prospects you can target precisely, through direct mail

6. prospects you can target loosely, through exhibitions, door-to-door marketing

7. prospects you can only target very broadly, through PR and media advertising such as TV, press and radio.

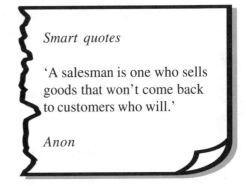

OK, now for the bad news. The number of prospects on your list is likely to arrange itself in the opposite order. In other words, you probably have a relatively small list of your own targets, a few more prospects on your list of customer recommendations, and so on, until you reach the bottom

Smart answers to tough questions

Q: Why would we ever bother to target the prospects who are least likely to respond?
A: We may already have approached the most promising prospects; those at the bottom of the list may be our only viable group. Even if they don't become customers this time, we may be able to move them into a more promising band of prospects ready for our *next* campaign.

of the list, where you can reach the highest number of prospects, albeit with the lowest return.

The prospects at the top of the list therefore give you the lowest cost per sale, and are your most promising targets for any new recruitment campaign. But they may not give you the numbers you are aiming for. In this case, you will need to move down the list, budgeting for a lower hit rate and a higher cost per sale as you go. This is one reason why you can't possibly budget for the campaign until you know how many new customers you are aiming to win. The cost of winning them is going to be heavily influenced by how far down the list you have to go to reach the number you are aiming for.

As a general rule, you should start at the top of your list where your costs are lowest; that's only common sense. However, this can give you a slightly insular customer base and in many industries you need to bring in fresh, new blood from time to time to top up your customer base. So don't automatically exclude the bottom end of the list on the sole grounds that it is more expensive – it may be worth it.

Profile your existing customers

If you're going to target prospects at the bottom end of your category list

– those least likely to buy – you'll need to decide who to direct your campaign at. Even at the top end of the list, where you may be targeting everyone who has been referred, or all your own list of promising prospects, you still need to decide how to approach them.

There's only one smart way to go about this: look at your existing customer list. You've gone to all the trouble of keeping detailed customer records; now use them. This is one of their most valuable benefits to you. Find out who normally buys your products or services. If most of your customers are under thirty-five, you can assume it's a good idea to target under thirty-fives again. If your customers all have in common an interest in home decorating, aim to target prospects with the same interests.

You can combine different sets of data from your existing customer base to give yourself a detailed profile of the kind of people who buy from you. Perhaps you'll find that the best prospects will be those who are under thirty-five, interested in home decorating, and have no children. Maybe the number of children doesn't seem to make much difference, but your customers tend to come from rural rather than urban areas.

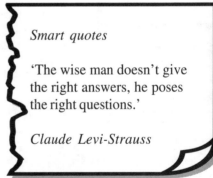

Smart quotes

'The wise man doesn't give the right answers, he poses the right questions.'

Claude Levi-Strauss

You will have sussed that the computer is not going to volunteer all this information unprompted. This is where you have to be smart in deciding which questions to ask it. Your own knowledge about your customers will give you clues, and you can follow up your hunches about which type of customers you think are buying your products. You may have simply gleaned an impression that most of your customers are in rural areas – asking the computer (for example using postcode selection) will confirm or refute this.

Taking this a stage further, you might have established in the past that most of your customers are under thirty-five but perhaps the over thirty-fives, although there are fewer of them, tend to spend more money with you. So the customer knowledge we discussed in the earlier chapters is essential when it comes to profiling your likely prospects.

The kind of areas you'll want to investigate when you are profiling your existing customers will include:

- socio-demographics

- location

- lifestyle

- behavior, such as value and frequency of orders.

For business customers, you'll need to consider:

- type of business

- size/turnover

- number of employees

- number and type of sites

- level of decision makers

- behavior, such as value and frequency of orders.

The customer's style of response

And there's more. As well as identifying which prospects are most likely to buy, you also want to know how best to approach them. Past recruitment campaigns should tell you this, as well as existing customers' responses to past offers. Do they tend to respond best to door-to-door marketing or to a phone call? Do they reply to press ads? When it comes to deciding how to approach your prospects, you'll need to know what has worked for you in the past.

You may find that your customers fall into different categories. Perhaps one type prefers to respond to direct mail, while another type is more likely to respond to magazine inserts. Maybe, if this is the case, you should run two different media campaigns directed at different groups of prospects. Certainly you need to know in order to be able to decide.

Responding to promotions isn't the only other consideration. You also need to consider where you found your existing customers. What is your track record for converting ex-customers back into customers? Or for getting enquirers to become customers? What usually works for you? If you have bought in

KILLER QUESTIONS

Shouldn't we try to understand *why* a prospect would choose to respond to one of our products if it was offered in one way, but not respond to the same offer made in another way?

mailing lists in the past, which ones have generated the best response? Which style of direct mail package works for you? And which kind of ad – color, size and so on? And in which publication?

Dredge up every bit of useful information about your existing customers to maximize the response to your new customer drive. And apply your own creativity to find the most promising lines of enquiry. The database is only as good as the use you put it to. So the better you know your existing customers, and the more skilled you are at finding the data on them, the higher response rate you will get to your campaign for new customers to add to the database.

Target your prospects

Once you have profiled your customers to establish what type of person or business is most likely to start buying from you, you have to decide which of these groups to target your campaign at. Will you direct it at the under thirty-fives with an interest in home decorating who aren't already customers? Or will you go for the over thirty-fives where the hit rate is lower, but each customer tends to be more valuable?

You may well go for more than one option, but your resources may prevent you from doing this. Two or more differing groups of prospects may need different approaches. Not only would you, for example, word a direct mail letter differently to each of them, but you might even need (going on past experience) to use a different medium for each. This has even more dramatic budget implications.

Most of the time, targeting stems from profiling your existing customers and then going out and recruiting more of the same. You may narrow this down to the most responsive group of customers, but you are seeking to increase your customer base without changing its profile. But there are times when this isn't possible:

- A new product or service may not be suited to your existing customers. Suppose you specialize in, for example, natural furnishing fabrics which are inexpensive – say, under £15 a meter. If you bring out a new line of luxury furnishing fabrics at over £50 a meter you could reasonably expect to attract a new type of customer. Your existing customers don't spend that kind of money on fabrics, so targeting more people who are like the customers you already have could be a big mistake.

- You may already have been through this process and identified all the prospects who resemble your existing customers, and targeted them in the past. If your customers come from a limited market, perhaps they are all UK paper manufacturers for example, you may have run out of new prospects in the same field. In this case you will have to look elsewhere. Perhaps outside the UK, or perhaps your product could be used in other industries.

You can almost always find new types of customers, but use the information you already have to do it. Be creative, but have a focus for your

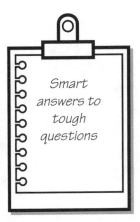

Smart answers to tough questions

Q: If we can't – or don't want to – recruit more customers like the ones we already have, what is the point of profiling our existing customers?
A: Any new customer is going to have something in common with our existing customers, even if it is only the thing which drives their shared need for our products or services. We need to find that common factor in order to direct our search for a new kind of customer.

SMART PEOPLE TO HAVE ON YOUR SIDE: RICHARD J. SCHONBERGER

- Author of *Building a Chain of Customers.*
- Early advocate of Japanese production techniques and approach to quality.
- Argues that Total Quality Management is too limited and inward-looking, and proposes a model which is focused on service to customers.

creativity. For example, one district council marketing department in the West of England was looking for ways to attract new tourists. The area was popular with cyclists, and the landscape was very flat. Many regular visitors to the area were cyclists who enjoyed a fairly level ride; not the type who wanted to cycle up mountains. The district council used this information creatively, and began to target cycling clubs in Holland, where the land is similarly flat. The campaign was highly successful, and the area now has a strong contingent of Dutch tourists.

So using data on existing customers doesn't mean you can only add more of the same customers. It simply means that however creative you are, you can still ensure a higher conversion rate of prospects into customers than you would without the data. Targeting Dutch cycling clubs was always going to generate a better response than targeting Alpine cycling clubs, for example.

As a general rule, the more precise your targeting, the greater will be your success rate at converting prospects into customers. You don't have to be that smart to see that if you target specifically under thirty-fives with a home-decorating bent and no children, and who live in a rural area, you will do better than if you aim simply at under thirty-fives (assuming your customer profiling is accurate). But things aren't always that easy, and there will be times when you have to have a fairly broad target group.

Plan your approach

Now you know who you want to make contact with, the next step is to decide how to make contact with them. And the smart way to do this is to focus on the prospect. What medium is most likely to:

- catch their attention?

- attract a response from them?

As always, the better you understand your customers, the more likely you are to know how to reach others like them. Of course, you have your research and your experience of past campaigns, but your own, personal understanding of your customers is still essential.

There's no point advertising on the radio if they never listen to it. Calling them on the phone isn't going to work well if they are in the kind of job where they are always away from their desk, perhaps on frequent business trips. Television ads which go out at six o'clock in the evening aren't going to reach busy working people who never leave the office before 7.00.

Even if you select the best medium, you may still need to pick the best way to use it. If your prospects *do* listen to the radio, you need to know which stations they listen to, and at what time of day. If they read women's magazines, are they more likely to linger over the fashion pages or the cookery pages? Dumb managers are inclined to think that if you choose the right kind of medium, you're there. But you have to be as specific as possible. Which day should the mailshot arrive to maximize the likelihood that they will read it? Which television programs do you want your ad to go out next to? When is a phone call most likely to catch them in without being inconvenient for them?

Smart quotes

'Advertising is what you do when you can't go to see somebody, that's all it is.'

Fairfax Cone

Many dumb managers choose the most promising medium (as they see it) and focus exclusively on that. Smart managers almost always end up using a combination of different media. They aim, for example, to make sure that by the time the mailshot arrives on the doormat, the prospect will already have seen the magazine ad or heard about your products on the radio.

There are plenty of media to choose from, and selecting the right ones is important. The main options are:

- direct mail

- door-to-door

- telephone

- television

- radio

- national press

- local press

- consumer magazines

- trade press

- inserts in packaging.

Going the direct route

If you are running a serious customer-recruitment campaign, you will need to use direct marketing. That is, marketing which demands a response from the prospect directly to you, rather than advertising which generally builds your brand image, or which encourages the customer to go anonymously into a shop and buy your product. You want to know who responds to your campaign, so make sure you invite a direct response to you.

What you don't want to do, however, is to be inundated with responses which will never lead to anything. So you also need to be smart about the kind of response you invite. Suppose you are an estate agent, specializing in unusual houses – converted lighthouses, that sort of thing. You could easily be deluged with responses from dreamers, who are never really going to buy one of these properties, but like to look at them so they can daydream about them.

Smart answers to tough questions

Q: So long as a customer is tempted to buy, why does it matter if they respond to the campaign this time or next time?

A: Customers who are tempted but don't respond are no use. We don't know who they are. We want to know who is tempted – that way we can tempt them that little bit more. And the sooner we get them on board, the sooner they will become profitable for us.

If you invite anyone to return a coupon and be added to your monthly mailing list of new properties, you'll be deluged with responses *and* you'll spend a fortune mailing people who are never going to buy. So communicate – and ask for a return communication – which will encourage the serious prospects while deterring those who are going to cost you money. There are plenty of ways of doing this; you will need to select the most effective one for your business. But to give you an example, you could ask people to phone in, and then filter them in the course of the phone calls. Or you could invite people to return a coupon in order to make an appointment – this deters people who are not genuine buyers.

Following up

Another way of getting the genuine prospects to identify themselves is to send out a brochure without a price list, or with only an outline price list, to everyone who responds to your campaign. This works in many industries, especially business to business. Those who are really interested will contact you again for detailed prices; those who don't get back in touch were clearly not that interested. (Be warned, however, that in some industries – especially if you sell to consumers – you risk their extreme irritation if you don't send out prices with your brochure. Reserve this technique for selling products for which genuine prospects won't care about the price, if you sell to consumers.)

It is important that at this stage of the planning process you think through how you are going to follow up the responses you expect to get. Different media attract a differing level of responses, with different final conversion rates. A magazine ad might attract a lot of initial response, with a high fallout rate at the next stage. Are you going to be able to cope with the response you are likely to get? Are you prepared to print and mail out that number of brochures? If you are inviting direct orders as a result of your campaign – as opposed to enquiries – can you fulfill all the likely orders in a reasonable time?

Initiate contact

The next step in the process of winning new customers is designing the communication itself: the advertisement, the mailshot, the TV ad, the insert or whatever. This is a job which dumb managers really like to get their teeth into. This, they think, is what winning customers is all about.

But it isn't. As a manager, the skill lies in being able to plan and oversee the whole process, and making sure that each step of the campaign is properly followed through. And, most importantly, you bring to the campaign your deep knowledge and understanding of the customer. Design skills are completely unnecessary. You only need to be able to recognize a good design when you see one.

This is the creative step in the campaign. And your job is to find good creative people – copywriters, graphic artists, photographers, designers – and let them do their stuff. To do their stuff well, however, they need you to give them a

> *Smart things to say about customers*
>
> As a manager, skills are less important than understanding. You can commission other people with skills, so long as you understand what they need to achieve.

clear brief. They need you to tell them exactly who this communication is aimed at. What sort of people are your prospects? What do they want to know about your products? What will persuade them to buy? Why would they buy *your* product or service rather than your competitors'?

Creativity doesn't happen in a vacuum. It is something which needs to be focused and channeled and sparked off by creating a medium in which it can flourish. You have to create that environment, by painting a vivid picture of the people this communication is aimed at. You do not, however, have to supply the creativity – just recognize it.

Smart quotes

'Curiosity about life in all of its aspects, I think, is still the secret of great creative people.'

Leo Burnett

And how do you recognize it? By understanding your customers and being able to put yourself in their shoes. If you were under thirty-five, enjoyed home decorating and so on, how would *you* feel if this fell through your letterbox, appeared on your TV screen, or in a magazine ad, or whatever? If you know your customers well enough to answer this question, you know how to recognize the kind of creative talent you need.

Keeping up appearances

Any kind of advertising, sales phone calls or other communications with prospects will inevitably have a strong impact on your branding and image. You must make sure that whatever communication you use, and however you design it, it reinforces your image rather than undermining it.

This means, for example, that if you promote a glossy, luxury image, you shouldn't send out a mailshot printed on cheap paper with low-quality photographs. If you sell gardening products aimed at people who live, or dream of living, in rural bliss with old-fashioned cottage gardens, any product shots with houses in the background should show rose-covered cottages and not suburban semis. If your organization has a strong reputation for friendly, knowledgeable service, any telephone sales staff – even if they are from an agency – should further this image rather than undermine it.

These are very basic examples; branding can sometimes be extremely subtle. The point is that you need to be very clear that the image you are promoting in your campaign is the same image you promote – and wish to promote – in everything else you do.

Create the customer

OK, that's all great, but where are the orders? The final stage in winning new customers is converting your prospects. There are books and books on the subject of selling, along with numerous seminars and training courses, correspondence courses and all the rest. But as a manager, you need to keep your eye on the bigger picture.

The first sale you make to a new customer is the most expensive. Often, you will have to operate at a loss for the first order – sometimes for the first few orders. This means that there is no point going through this entire process only to lose the customer after the first sale or two – which is precisely what will happen if you don't live up to your promises. So don't make promises you can't keep. Treat your prospects with the same integrity you treat your customers with.

If your after-sales service turns out to be no good, or the product doesn't come up to the standard you gave the customer to believe that it would, or if your accounts department cock up the invoicing, or the production department forget to add the customized alterations, or the delivery department sends the order to the wrong address ... you have probably lost a customer. Not only that, but you've lost a customer that you never made any profit out of in the first place.

Your newest customers are your most vulnerable. You have had less chance to show them how wonderful you are, and less opportunity to build up their loyalty. These customers – the ones which have least justified their existence in terms of being profitable – are the ones most likely to desert you.

So you need to invest extra effort – and make sure everyone else invests a special effort too – into encouraging your new customers to feel fully committed to you as soon as possible. As soon as your prospects convert into customers, give them the full customer treatment – the high level of service, the attention, the respect and all the rest of it that your long standing customers already know they can rely on you for.

However focused you may be on the campaign to recruit new customers, don't lose sight of the fact that once the prospect converts, it is not the end of the process but the start of a long and profitable relationship. So your six steps to winning new customers are in fact six steps which lead to the beginning of something, not to an end result at all:

1. set your objectives

2. profile your existing customers

3. target your prospects

4. plan your approach

5. initiate contact

6. create the customer.

8

Out There

So what's new? Customers have been around for thousands of years but ways of understanding and dealing with them are still developing rapidly – more now than ever before. As customers become more demanding, and our ability to give them what they want increases, so their expectations of what we will give them in the future are raised. So where are our customer service programs and techniques going to go over the next few years?

The Internet revolution

There is a popular view that the Internet is the new medium of the 21st century. Without a strong Internet presence you can't hope to compete in the brave new world of the future. But is it really true? Certainly the majority of organizations now have a Web site, so they clearly subscribe to the overall premise.

Smart quotes

'The best way to predict the future is to create it.'

Peter Drucker

KILLER QUESTIONS

How can the Internet possibly live up to all the hype, if it is nothing but an electronic method of delivering our brochure to prospects?

But do you ever have a sneaking suspicion that all this hype is just a case of the emperor's new clothes? Everyone wants a Web site because everyone else has got one, and they don't want to be left out? Does it actually help business? Take your own organization as an example. Assuming you have a Web site, what did it cost to set up, and how much does it cost to run? And set against that, how much extra business is it bringing in? In most organizations, the answer to these questions would show that the figures don't really add up. Web sites are costing a lot of organizations a lot of money, but they daren't abandon them because ... well, because cyberspace is the market place of the future, isn't it?

So is there a solution, or are we all just going to go on pouring money into the Net? Well, to find the answer to this you have to think in terms of your customers. Too many organizations set up a Web site and then wonder what to put on it. The obvious answer appears to be to use it as a showcase for their products and services. So they do this. The Web site becomes, in effect, a hi-tech catalogue. Maybe they try to attract more people to the site by including a regular newsletter or magazine. But, in essence, the Web site is a tool for providing information.

Smart things
to say about customers

The Web site as an information source only will never be more than a glorified catalogue, however glossily it is presented.

Clothing the emperor

So how does the customer feel? Did they want an information source on the Net to save them ringing up for a catalogue? And does visiting a supplier's Web site make them feel more loyal to that supplier? We need to know what customers really want from our Web site before we launch it, otherwise we not only waste a lot of money, but we also risk frustrating our customers if we don't offer them what they actually want.

You will obviously have to ask your own customers what they really want from you, but recent research has thrown up a lot of answers to what Internet customers in general want from Web sites. And the answers go much of the way towards explaining why it is that Web sites aren't more profitable. If you take note of these findings, and add them to your own customer research, you should be able to find out how to make the Internet really work for your organization ... while your competitors get left behind.

- Who visits your Web site? In most cases, your existing customers, not your prospects. A big concern for Internet users is trust and confidence in an organization. Without this, they are reluctant to use your Web site. Prospects have not built up such trust with you, but existing customers have. In surveys, not only do most Internet users indicate that they are more positive about dealing on the Net with suppliers they already know, they are also more likely to have a positive attitude to a site than non-customers.

- Personal information. The key to good customer service, especially in relationship marketing, is information about the customer. So will they give it to you on the Internet? Apparently not – at least, not happily. Even existing customers would rather give you personal information via some other medium. This resistance can be softened if you give them an inducement, such as improved service. But don't expect as good a response to requests for personal information via the Net as you would get by traditional post or phone approaches.

With relationship marketing becoming the new style of dealing with customers, it will become essential to be able to persuade Internet users to part with personal information. One of the key ways to do this is to explain why the information is useful – from the customer's point of view – and how it will be used. Trading this information off for recognized benefits will be key; for example, showing how giving the information will lead to faster delivery or improved service of some kind.

- Using e-mail. Now here's something Internet users *are* enthusiastic about. In fact, it looks as though the trend may be towards using e-mail instead of the telephone, since it is so convenient. Not only is it quick, but it is less intrusive for the customer, who can access it whenever it suits them. It may well be that, in the future, call centres will have far fewer phone calls to answer – but more e-mails to deal with. Consumers do not, however, appreciate junk e-mail, so e-mail needs to be seen to be relevant by the recipient.

> **Smart things to say about customers**
>
> If people are reluctant to give us the information we want, we have to look for ways to persuade them it's worth their while. Once they have made that decision, future information should be far easier to elicit.

And now for the discouraging news – at least for customers. In traditional media, customers prefer replies to enquiries in the same form in which they submitted them. So if they phone, they like a phone call back. If they write to an organization, they want the response by post. It is hardly surprising, then, that e-mail users feel the same way. They want their response by e-mail. Doesn't seem unreasonable does it? But do they get it? Recent research showed that over 40 percent of companies didn't reply to e-mails at all. Of those that did reply, almost half responded by post. The lesson should be clear. Internet users prefer to communicate via e-mail, and they want your response by e-mail, too.

- What about new customers? Although most people who visit your site will be regular customers, of course Internet users do also visit new sites. So how do they feel about them? The evidence is that existing customers are relatively tolerant of failings in Web sites, but that new prospects are much more easily put off. This is partly because existing customers know you well enough to be able to find the information they want more easily, and more likely to phone you if they *do* encounter problems. The most frustrating problems for new customers are poor search functions or incomplete information.

Although new prospects may visit your Web site, they are far less likely to place an order or to give you any personal information if they have found your site for themselves. You need them to have heard of you before they visit and to trust you with their details – including credit card details. In general, you need to build an image of trust – or have already established one – outside the Internet before you can realisti-cally hope to persuade new prospects to interact with you. The best reputation of all to have with new prospects is word-of-mouth recom-mendation. Hard though it is, some organizations – such as Amazon.com

Smart
answers to
tough
questions

Q: If we are trustworthy as an organization, why shouldn't new prospects do business with us?
A: It isn't enough to be trustworthy. We must be seen and believed to be a business they can trust. And that means focusing all our traditional mar-keting efforts on building an image of trustworthiness if we want cus-tomers to do business with us on the Net.

for example – do manage to create a trustworthy brand through word of mouth alone.

Word of mouth is increasingly popular as a method of finding new suppliers. Consumers are becoming cynical about advertising, and are much more likely to ask friends and colleagues for recommendations than they used to be. What is more, some research suggests that customers who visit Web sites are nearly four times as likely to pass on word-of-mouth recommendations as those who don't visit the Web site. This makes a good Web site a valuable means of publicizing the company via the best method possible – word of mouth. But be warned: if your Web site generates a negative response in those who visit it, this is also more likely to be passed on.

All of this evidence suggests that most organizations are missing the point when it comes to using the Internet. It *does* have great potential as the medium of the future, but only if businesses stop following the herd. The smart managers are beginning to notice that the herd is getting it wrong.

Another interesting line of research has compared what organizations with Web sites consider makes for a good Web site with what Internet users say makes a good Web site. The results show, if nothing else, that most of the companies can't ever have tried asking Internet users what they actually want. So what do companies with Web sites think are the constituents of a good Web site:

- It should look good.

- It is ideal for niche marketing.

- It is a way to give our customers and prospects information about our products and services.

- It supports other advertising in building the strength of our brand image.

And here's the information that dumb managers need but have never thought to ask for: the consumers view of what constitutes a good Web site:

- It should be easy and quick to use.

- It doesn't work for niche marketing – everyone can access the site, and those whom it isn't aimed at simply find it impossible to use.

- We aren't so interested in collecting information; what we really want is to be able to place orders online.

- We don't want Web sites which are just advertising, however clever or gimmicky. We use the Net because we have a specific need we want met – to satisfy a query or place an order, for example.

It is becoming clear that one of the current problems in Web site design is that organizations are employing the wrong kind of people to create their Internet presence for them. Most organizations are using design companies

SMART PEOPLE
TO HAVE ON
YOUR SIDE:

ROSABETH
MOSS KANTER

SMART PEOPLE TO HAVE ON YOUR SIDE: ROSABETH MOSS KANTER

- Academic and author of *Change Masters* and *When Giants Learn to Dance*.
- Believes that successful change depends on an 'integrative' rather than 'segmentalist' organizational structure.

or brand advertising agencies to design their sites for them; yet these companies generally have no knowledge of the broader marketing issues which the Internet encompasses. They may be able fulfil all the requirements which organizations have – according to the survey responses we have just seen – but they don't understand the issues which we have just established matter to the consumer.

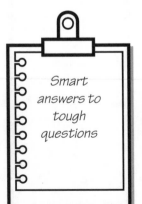

Smart things to say about customers

If we want our Web site to be an integrated and central part of our whole future marketing operation, we have to design it with that whole purpose in mind.

Serducts and provices

Here's another fascinating trend in customer service. Many product companies are finding that it is increasingly difficult to come up with new products which will have a lifetime long enough to be worthwhile. Meantime, many service companies have a different problem; they are increasingly aware that their only true assets are their staff. If they were to go – taking their expertise along with them to competing organizations – the company is left with nothing worth selling.

And strangely enough, many of these companies are finding the same solution and – like so many of today's customer service solutions – the change is being driven by new technology; in many cases the Internet.

Product companies are catching on to the fact that services often last longer, and are easier to upgrade as the new technology develops, than products. So they are finding new ways to add value to their products by adding

Smart answers to tough questions

Q: New technology is changing so fast; all our products are obsolete almost before we've launched them. How can we stay ahead of the game?

A: Maybe we should look elsewhere for a competitive edge, and devise services instead of products which can give us the extra desirability we need in the customers' eyes.

services. Take car manufacturers as an example. They used to sell cars, plain and simple. Now, however, they package their cars up with services such as warranties, service guarantees and even finance plans, all adding value to the basic product.

On the other side of the coin, service companies are looking for ways to develop products which will use the expertise of their people. That way, even if the people move on, the company still has a valuable commodity to sell. So if a communications consultancy offers its customers software which will help them to produce their own magazine, they are offering a product to go alongside the service they provide.

You can't see the join

As this productizing of services and servicizing of products becomes more sophisticated, more and more companies are offering combinations of the two which defy categorizing as either products or services. These hybrid product/services are becoming increasingly prolific, and are largely driven by new technology. Here are a few examples:

- a computer consultancy which enables its customers to download 'freeware' from its Web site which helps them to manage their computer more effectively

- a training consultancy producing one-to-one training software available to clients via their Web site

- an accountancy business whose Web site allows clients to submit their accounts for automated auditing.

Combining products and services is the trend of the future for adding value. Increasingly, businesses who want to maximize customer service and satisfaction will be looking for ways to produce these hybrids, rather than limiting themselves to the old-fashioned *either/or* thinking. Smart managers need to learn to think in this new, broader way in order to find new ways to satisfy customers and build closer relationships with them.

Talking to your customers face-to-face

Virtually all the big changes happening in customer service over the next few years and beyond will be driven by new technology; and if you're smart, that's where you'll focus your mind to find new innovations which will put you ahead of the competition. But the Internet isn't the only place to look for ideas.

Another promising area for customer service development is the telephone. Once upon a time you picked up the phone, dialled the person you wanted to speak to, held the conversation and then put the phone down. Now, however, there is a wealth of options. You can talk to several people at once, you can book a meeting over the phone, and you can even see the person you're talking to as you speak – videoconferencing in other words.

SMART PEOPLE TO HAVE ON YOUR SIDE:

ROBERT LEIDERMAN AND SIMON RONCORONI

SMART PEOPLE TO HAVE ON YOUR SIDE: ROBERT LEIDERMAN AND SIMON RONCORONI

- Consultants in strategic telephone marketing.
- Pioneered carelines in the UK.
- Champion the telephone as a prime tool for customer service.

But it's not only people you can see when you hold a videoconference. You can see whatever the camera is pointed at. And some organizations are finding terrific applications for this which create huge leaps in customer service and in relationship building with customers.

The best way to illustrate this is with an example. Hartness International is an American manufacturing company. They make case packers, which are the machines that put bottles into boxes ready for shipping. If these case packers break down, it can be seriously bad news for the customer. Their bottling line comes to a standstill. A 24-hour delay in repairing the case packer can cost the customer hundreds of thousands of dollars.

Hartness aren't happy about this; customer service is a top priority for them. But they are based in the middle of nowhere. When the company was started in the 1970s, they had a policy that they would employ only service technicians who held a pilot's licence. That way, they could reach their customers far quicker to perform repairs on any machines that needed it.

But as time went on, taking a few hours to reach a customer became less acceptable. Hartness wanted to reduce the downtime for each customer when the machines hit problems. In fact, they wanted to be on the spot as soon as the machine broke down. And then, in the mid-90s, they saw the solution: videoconferencing. It would mean they could see the machines, diagnose the problem and direct the repairs without having to leave their head office.

There was a hitch, however. Although videoconferencing had been developed, it didn't allow you to see just anything, anywhere in the building. You could see the directors sitting in the boardroom, but it was another matter to go down to the shop floor where there were no telephones around. Undeterred, Hartness could see that the technology was perfectly possible; it just didn't happen to exist yet.

So they invented it. They developed the Video Response System (VRS) which they now, incidentally, sell to all sorts of companies who don't even use their case packers. More immediately, however, they could use VRS to direct live repairs as soon as a machine malfunctioned.

Obviously, this created an immediate boost in customer service because it meant that delays through machine failure were drastically cut. But it produced other benefits too:

SMART PEOPLE TO HAVE ON YOUR SIDE:

PHILIP CROSBY

- The customer's own technicians physically repair the fault. This in effect trains them to understand the machines better; it acts as a coaching session. The machine also stores a video of each repair so if the same fault repeats, the customer's technicians simply play it back to repeat the repair. Hartness are training their customers to help themselves – that's customer service.

- VRS may have been developed to help repair machines, but Hartness have found that the VRS service is a huge bonus when it comes to selling their machinery. This is yet another example of a product being tied

---

SMART PEOPLE TO HAVE ON YOUR SIDE: PHILIP CROSBY

- Quality guru, one-time corporate vice president of ITT.
- Author of *Quality is Free* and *Quality without Tears*.
- Invented the concept of 'zero defects'.

in with a service which is as strong a selling point as the original product.

Focus on the customer

A recent survey of senior marketing people by the Marketing Council asked them what they thought were the most essential areas of marketing to focus on until the year 2005. Focusing on customers – not just market segments – was clearly the top priority. The responses were:

Increased customer focus	59%
Creativity/innovation	34%
Quality	21%
Vision	15%
Integration	8%

So the two key lessons for being smart in the future are: exploit the new technology, and focus on the customer as an individual. Combine these two, and find ways to use new technology to drive the improvements in your service to customers. Be prepared to change your department and your organization dramatically. Make yourself indispensable to your customers, increase the value of each customer to you, and remember that your own greatest skill lies in not just knowing but truly understanding your customers.

Smart quotes

'If an organization is to meet the challenges of a changing world, it must be prepared to change everything about itself except beliefs as it moves through corporate life ... The only sacred cow in an organization should be its basic philosophy of doing business.'

Thomas Watson Jr

Index